Approaches to Ethics in Higher Education

Teaching Ethics across the Curriculum

Approaches to Ethics in Higher Education

Teaching Ethics across the Curriculum

Prepared for the **ETHICS** Project by Susan Illingworth. Illustrations by Susan Illingworth.

A partnership of the LTSN subject centres for Philosophical and Religious Studies, UKCLE, LTSN-01, Psychology, Bioscience and Health Sciences & Practice

© PRS-LTSN, 2004

Published by the Philosophical and Religious Studies Subject Centre,
Learning and Teaching Support Network (PRS-LTSN)
School of Theology and Religious Studies
University of Leeds
Leeds LS2 9JT

First Published March 2004

ISBN 0-9544524-2-9

Printed in Wales by Cambrian Printers, Aberystwth.

Contents

Foreword

David Gosling

Critical Change Consultants for Higher Education

All education has an ethical dimension, but for an increasing number of students ethics is becoming an essential part of their curriculum. At a time when there is considerable media interest in issues relating to professional ethics and ethical questions in research, this is an expanding area of the curriculum in universities and colleges. The ethics of stem-cell research, genetically modified foods, cloning, vivisection, post-mortem use of organs, all of these and many others have become highly political questions. Equally, nurses, and the professions allied to medicine, teachers, social workers, lawyers, psychologists all face difficult ethical issues in their work. Most professions now have codes of professional ethics—sometimes developed as a response to public criticism of the behaviour of a minority of practitioners—which practitioners must interpret and use to guide their actions.

Since a degree qualification is an essential prerequisite for entry into all professions, it is clear that higher education cannot afford to ignore this aspect of the preparation for professionals. But there is a more general argument for including ethics in the curriculum. Helping students to reflect on and deal with the ethical issues they will face in their careers is an essential part of any vocational training. The growth of work-based learning in, for example, vocationally oriented Foundation Degrees, suggests that there will be a growing need to investigate and support ways of teaching ethics in a wider variety of subjects in more diverse learning environments at all levels of higher education.

The ETHICS project has demonstrated that there is a clear and growing interest in teaching ethics. The project has been timely and significant. Many HE staff have not received training in the teaching of ethics, but are called-on to organise and promote the learning of students in these sensitive and complex areas. There is nervousness sometimes about not wishing to impose answers, and yet the public demands ever higher standards of ethical behaviour from professionals.

This booklet is one of the outcomes of the ETHICS project. It brought together staff teaching in law, medicine, health professions, psychology and biosciences with teachers of philosophy and religious studies to exchange views about how to approach the teaching of ethics. The inter-disciplinary nature of the project has been one of its key characteristics, enabling knowledge and experience to be shared across six disciplinary areas.

A very encouraging start has been made in identifying the issues in ethics teaching and sharing some solutions to the concerns of teachers of ethics, but there is much more still to do. In just over a year the ETHICS project cannot complete all the work that would be of value to the sector and ways of continuing this debate within the new Higher Education Academy need to be actively pursued. The project has demonstrated the potential for collaborative work across a number of subject centres and it is to be hoped that the Academy will also support this kind of interdisciplinary development in the future.

The success of this project has been the result not only of those staff in the LTSN subject centres who have been convinced of its value and have worked to achieve its objectives, but also because of the contribution of teachers of ethics in HEIs across the country. I hope that these teachers of ethics will continue to demonstrate this commitment so that the issues raised in this book will continue to be debated and experience shared. If this happens then students will reap the benefit of having better prepared and more reflective teachers of ethics.

Acknowledgements

With thanks to all workshop participants, Project Officers, Jackie Wilson for feedback and comments, Karen Taylor Burge for information on Professional Codes, David Mossley for substantial editorial work in preparing the text and cartoons for publication and all the reviewers.

Introduction

The ETHICS Project was a one year initiative funded by the LTSN[1]. Its primary aim was the collective examination of the current provision of applied/professional ethics teaching within Higher Education (HE) to identify key concerns and to facilitate the sharing of good practice.

This guide forms part of the Project's output. It is hoped that it will provide a useful resource not only for new teachers of ethics looking for ideas on course development, but also for experienced ethicists for whom it will provide a 'snapshot' of current teaching and learning priorities.

Who Needs to Learn About Ethics?

Society is empowered by ever-improving access to more and more information, and is demanding greater transparency and accountability. [2]

Perhaps the best reason for studying ethics is a strong personal interest in the subject matter but the requirement to teach ethics is a growing one throughout HE. Many departments whose main academic interests lie elsewhere are now making room within their curricula for an introduction to the moral issues germane to their primary discipline.

The pressure to teach ethics comes from benchmarking statements, the requirements of professional associations, and the more general drive to provide students with key transferable skills. What these sources have in common is the idea that students need to study ethics in order to meet the expected demands of their working lives. HE can only meet this need effectively if it tailors the learning and teaching environment to the requirements of different student groups so that students see ethics as:

- Relevant to their primary discipline.
- A subject that they can tackle with confidence, and with the expectation of attaining an acceptable level of expertise.

All links are available live at http://www.prs-ltsn.ac.uk/ethics

[1] Learning and Teaching Support Network, part of the Higher Education Academy: **http://www.heacademy.ac.uk/**

[2] The British Council (2000) *Science and Society: Towards a Democratic Science,* **http://www.britcoun.org/science1/intro.htm**

When our graduates leave university they will increasingly be asked to discuss moral issues competently and constructively with a diverse range of people. In some cases they will be asked to address the concerns of members of the public. One of the primary motives behind the drive towards a greater ethical awareness among graduates is an appreciation of the consequences for any profession of a loss of public confidence. It will therefore be increasingly important for teachers of ethics to produce learning and teaching outcomes on three levels:

- Subject-specific: students will need to understand:
    - The moral issues that arise most frequently within their own subject area.
    - The perspectives of students and professionals within this subject area.
    - The perspectives of key stakeholders/service users in the professions served by that subject area.
- Interprofessional: students will need to understand the perspectives of people from professionally related subject areas on issues of shared moral significance.
- Public: students will need to understand the perspectives of private individuals and relevant social groups on moral issues arising within their subject area.

The third level, based on the need for public accountability, is potentially the most complex and challenging of all and is likely to increase in importance as internet access grows. From official sources such as the Home Office's pages on the use of Animals in Scientific Procedures[3] through the Research Councils[4] and bodies such as the Nuffield Council on Bioethics[5] to national and international campaigning organisations such as Greenpeace[6] and the Worldwide Fund for Nature,[7] people can inform themselves on ethically sensitive matters and involve themselves in public debate more readily than ever before. Any graduate entering a profession which has attracted public

---

All links are available live at http://www.prs-ltsn.ac.uk/ethics

[3] http://www.homeoffice.gov.uk/comrace/animals/reference.html#

[4] See The Welcome Trust's Biomedical Ethics Programme at http://www.wellcome.ac.uk/en/1/pinbio.html and the MRC's Centre for Best Practice for Animals in Research at http://www.mrc.ac.uk/index/public-interest/public-ethics_and_best_practice/public-use_of_animals_in_research/public-cbpar.htm

[5] http://www.nuffieldbioethics.org/home/

[6] http://www.greenpeace.org.uk

[7] http://www.wwf.org.uk/core/index.asp

interest or concern must therefore be prepared to discuss ethical issues on a peer-to-peer basis with those who do not share their professional perspective.

While many academic disciplines must respond to societal changes and be sensitive to public opinion, few can rival professional ethics for the dynamism and immediacy of its relationship with external factors. This often makes it a rewarding area in which to work but it can also mean operating within a learning and teaching environment which is in such a constant state of flux that everyone has to run merely to stand still. The aim of this guide is to hold up a mirror to ethics learning and teaching across the curriculum so that teachers can get a clearer idea of the dominant themes and concerns, and locate their own practice within the context of a cross-disciplinary spectrum.

Approaches

An 'approach' in this context refers to the *'point or direction from which one views … a subject of inquiry'.*[8]

Teachers of applied or professional ethics may use a variety of methods over the course of a module, but the context in which students first encounter ethics influences their perception of the subject and its relationship to professional values and behaviour. The next three chapters outline three commonly used approaches to ethics. For the purposes of this guide these different 'ways in' have been designated the pragmatic , embedded and theoretical approaches.

The **pragmatic** approach takes as its starting point the framework of rules and procedures defined by regulatory bodies charged with the task of raising or maintaining professional standards. When students leave Higher Education to begin work they will enter a world in which professional propriety and accountability are of increasing importance. Codes of conduct are already widespread within health and social care, and are now influencing commercial practice (for example through The Institute of Business Ethics[9] which offers detailed guidance on Codes of Ethics within business). Most students will need to be aware that such codes exist, and able to apply them to their own behaviour. Students who are required to do a research project as part of their coursework, or who are likely to find employment in research-oriented professions will also have good reason to acquire some familiarity with Research Ethics Committees and the factors that influence their deliberations. Learning and teaching that starts from the student's 'need to know'

All links are available live at http://www.prs-ltsn.ac.uk/ethics

[8] *Oxford English Dictionary* (online version) **http://dictionary.oed.com/**

[9] **http://www.ibe.org.uk/home.html**

in these and related areas is pragmatic in the sense that ethical considerations are defined in relation to their practical consequences for the student.

The **embedded** approach also involves the notion of professionalism but in a very different way. Where the pragmatic approach concentrates on professionalism as behaviour constrained by an agreed code of conduct, the embedded approach interprets it in terms of the students' emerging sense of self-identity. Modules in which students are introduced to ethics in an 'embedded' way present moral issues holistically, as an integral part of some broader area of concern which has a significant ethical dimension such as Fitness for Practice. The sense of self-identity fostered by embedded methods can be expanded readily to accommodate the idea of the professional as part of a multi-disciplinary team, which makes it a useful approach for interdisciplinary courses. A further difference between pragmatic and embedded methods is that while the former sees ethics primarily as a set of externally imposed constraints, the embedded approach places a greater emphasis on personal autonomy.

The third approach has been called **theoretical**, because, unlike pragmatic and embedded methods, it places an understanding of moral theory at the heart of ethics learning and teaching. Students introduced to ethics via this approach first encounter it as a theoretical discipline, by examining key moral theories, principles and concepts and subjecting them to critical appraisal. The ethics of real-life or life-like situations are then presented in terms of the application of that theory. The theoretical approach has the longest history in Higher Education for it is the one adopted by departments of Philosophy for which ethics has always been a core subject. It provides students with a good basis for a critical evaluation of the moral issues germane to their subject area and also develops their capacity to present reasoned, structured and coherent arguments. It encourages an objective viewpoint, in contrast to the pragmatic and embedded approaches where students are encouraged to see ethics first and foremost as an aspect of their own professional behaviour and interpersonal relations. However, an emphasis on theory and role distance can make ethics seem irrelevant and inaccessible for some students who might have difficulty seeing the connection between theory and their own everyday practice.

Each of the above three approaches is supported by a case study, illustrating the ways in which case studies can be adapted to serve a range of learning and teaching methods and objectives. The deployment of case studies is expanded upon in the **Appendix** (p. 93).

This Guide also considers a number of factors affecting the creation of a supportive learning environment, tailored to the special challenges posed by applied and professional ethics. These issues are not specific to individual approaches, and may be of relevance to any ethics module.

The closing section considers the future of ethics learning and teaching in Higher Education, and argues for interdisciplinary collaboration between ethical theorists and those with expertise in its subject-specific application.

An online version of this guide, with links to the ETHICS Project's Case Study database and other resources can be found at:

http://www.prs-ltsn.leeds.ac.uk/ethics/

Approaches to Ethics Teaching

The ETHICS Project's review of the current status of ethics in Higher Education suggested that there are three commonly used 'ways in' to the subject and that this might be a useful way to categorise the different kinds of learning and teaching offered.

Pragmatic

Introduction

The pragmatic approach takes as its starting point the framework of rules and procedures defined by regulatory bodies charged with the task of raising or maintaining professional standards. It is pragmatic in the sense that these ethical considerations are defined in relation to their practical consequences for the student.

As future professionals students have an interest in avoiding censure, and a pragmatically oriented ethics module can help them to do this by first alerting them to the many professional codes of conduct in operation, and then helping them to understand how these codes might be applied to their own behaviour.

Similarly, as researchers, their research proposals may need Research Ethics Committee (REC) approval and it will save time and effort on their part if they can anticipate and accommodate any ethical concerns that might be raised.

The advantage of introducing students to ethics in this way is that it is easy for them to appreciate its relevance to their main area of interest but they need not see ethics purely in terms of external constraint. Modules can help them acquire some understanding of the principles and moral arguments used in the formulation of codes of conduct or which underpin the deliberations of a Research Ethics Committee. Learning and teaching can also facilitate the student's internalisation of the values inherent in those moral principles and arguments. In these cases teaches will often combine the pragmatic approach with the methods described in the theoretical and embedded approaches. However, this does not always happen in practice and for some students in Higher Education, their experience of ethics learning and teaching will be largely confined to a pragmatic agenda. Helping students acquire knowledge of professional/research standards and the ability to apply them is therefore one way in which benchmarked requirements to teach ethics are currently being interpreted.

Ethics teaching structured around the pragmatic approach is often incorporated into modules whose primary learning objectives are drawn from the students' main area of study. Delivery of the ethics component will therefore tend to be adapted to the needs of the parent learning and teaching methodology. For example, within science faculties coverage of REC approval may be incorporated into general guidance on final-year undergraduate research projects; this guidance will be concerned mainly to advise the students on the selection of an appropriate topic, supervision arrangements, access to laboratory facilities, scheduling of their workload, and so on. Ethics provision will comprise advice on the features of a research project that are likely to require REC approval such as the use of human or animal subjects, accompanied by details of the internal procedure for obtaining such approval. This material will often be supported by copies of the RECs guidelines and, where appropriate, any guidance provided by the relevant professional body. This means that, in contrast to the embedded and theoretical approaches, the learning and teaching methods employed within the pragmatic approach are more varied, and in some cases less suited to the specific needs of the ethics-oriented learning and teaching objectives of the module.

Teaching that focuses on the requirements of professional codes and/or REC procedures must be directly responsive to external factors. Learning and teaching materials will therefore need to be revised continuously to ensure that they reflect the standards currently in force. The remainder of this chapter offers a brief review of Professional Codes of Practice to identify the common moral concerns embedded in them, followed by an outline of the current system of Research Ethics Committee approval. Both areas are too complex to be covered in detail in a guide of this nature, and the main aim of these sections is to identify sources of information for teachers, most of them internet-based. Given the rapidly evolving nature of the legislation and its associated executive and administrative structures, the internet is the most effective (and in many cases the only practicable) way of communicating up-to-date information. Web page addresses are given for all the sources of information cited, but when accessing multiple links please view the online version of this Guide, from which the sources can be accessed via hyperlinks from the main text.

This section also includes two guest contributions. The first is from Bryan Vernon, Lecturer in Ethics of Health Care, University of Newcastle-upon-Tyne, and draws on his experience as a contributor to a range of Clinical Ethics Advisory Committees. Clinical Ethics Committees are modelled on the advisory and regulatory model of the Research Ethics Committee, adapted to the needs of clinical practice. The functions of the Clinical Ethics Committee can be divided into three broad areas:

1) Provision of ethics input into Trust Policy and Guidelines
2) Support for health professionals in individual cases
3) Facilitation of ethics education for health professionals and other Trust staff.

This categorisation was taken from the UK Clinical Ethics Network website, a new online resource which offers a registration facility for Clinical Ethics Committees, examples of the range of work carried out and an issues list, showing the topics that committees have discussed most frequently.[10] Rev. Vernon provides valuable insight into the qualities needed to be an effective member of such a committee.

The second contribution comes from Diane Beale, Senior Research Fellow at the University of Nottingham. Her article offers a detailed description of the management of the ethical implications of applied research and teaching within Nottingham's Institute of Work, Health & Organisations. She argues that students should be encouraged to "think ethically" rather than simply apply a code or set of standards.

The final part of this section will present a case study illustrating the pragmatic approach.

Professional Codes of Practice

Many graduates will work in areas that do not relate directly to their area of study. Accordingly, most benchmark statements avoid reference to individual professional codes, but rather require that students:

- Understand the need for such codes
- Are able to apply them.

In faculties such as those of Law, Medicine or Healthcare the relevant professional codes can be identified more readily. For example, the Law Society provides a detailed online guide to the Professional conduct of solicitors, including advice on discrimination, conflicts of interest and confidentiality. [11]

In healthcare, professional codes will often be of immediate relevance as many students have some experience of clinical practice before graduating. However, work experience will increasingly take place within the context of an interdisciplinary team and this has resulted in some institutions structuring ethics learning and teaching around an Interprofessional Education (IPE) framework (see section p. 38 for a discussion of ethics and IPE). Where classes bring together students from more than one discipline, there will be more than one applicable professional code.

The number of Codes of Practice or Conduct applicable within healthcare alone is vast. For example, within Medicine, the General Medical Council defines fourteen key principles in the *Duties of a*

All links are available live at http://www.prs-ltsn.ac.uk/ethics

[10] http://www.ethics-network.org.uk/

[11] http://www.guide-on-line.lawsociety.org.uk/

Doctor, with associated guidance on their interpretation and application.[12] Individual specialities may then have their own representative bodies such as The Royal College of Paediatrics and Child Health which defines a set of duties answering the particular needs of their field[13] or the Association of Anaesthetists of Great Britain and Ireland which provides a code of conduct for anaesthetists involved in private practice.[14] For Nursing and Midwifery a new Nursing and Midwifery Council Code of Conduct came into effect in June 2002.[15]

Paramedical professions have their own codes. For example, the General Osteopathic Council's Code of Practice lays down standard expected of registered osteopaths,[16] while the Chartered Society of Physiotherapy specifies rules of conduct intended 'to reflect the reasonable behaviour expected of a physiotherapist as a *professional*.[17] For pharmacists, the UK Medicines Information (UKMI) online service provides a basic introduction to the function of NHS RECs, the role of pharmacists on these RECs and the procedure to gaining REC approval.[18]

Non-clinical staff are also covered, as in the Code of Conduct for NHS Managers[19] or the College of Health Care Chaplains Code of Conduct.[20]

Despite this apparent complexity, an examination of the codes will reveal a number of recurrent themes, applicable across many disciplines, both inside and outside healthcare. Their main objective is to prohibit behaviour likely to bring the profession into disrepute or undermine public confidence in it, and they do this by stressing a number of key qualities. Ethics learning and teaching that takes its starting point from professional codes of practice can therefore be based around a consideration of these themes. By so doing it will prepare students to apply the key requirements of most professional codes to their own behaviour.

The first group of qualities relates to what might loosely be called 'professionalism'. Professionals are expected to act with integrity, a complex notion that usually comprises such things as honesty, an avoidance of plagiarism, avoidance (or at least reporting) of any conflicts of interest and a willingness to report colleagues suspected of professional misconduct. The importance of working

---

All links are available live at http://www.prs-ltsn.ac.uk/ethics

[12] http://www.gmc-uk.org/standards/default.htm

[13] http://www.rcpch.ac.uk/about/duties.html

[14] http://www.aagbi.org/IPC_codeofpractice.html

[15] http://www.nmc.uk.org/nmc/main/publications/codeOfProfessionalConduct.pdf

[16] http://www.osteopathy.org.uk/goc/council/code.shtml

[17] http://www.csp.org.uk/thecsp/rulesofconduct/rulesofprofessionalconduct.cfm

[18] http://www.ukmi.nhs.uk/Research/Ethics.asp

[19] http://www.publications.doh.gov.uk/nhsmanagerscode/codeofconduct.pdf

[20] http://www.lichfield.anglican.org/healthcarechaplains/code.htm

within the law is stressed by most codes, and teachers might find it useful to combine teaching that refers to specific professional codes with coverage of any associated legal obligations. Service-oriented professions also have a general requirement that their members should provide a good standard of care. Both professionalism and the duty of care will also be considered in the next section of this guide which deals with the embedded approach to ethics learning and teaching. Professions operating through private practice also have defined duties of financial propriety. Apart from activities such as fraud and embezzlement, which would be covered by the obligation to act at all times within the law, codes pay specific attention to advertising, which must be accurate (for example, by not making false or inflated claims about the services one provides). Professions which offer an advisory service to the public or other professionals may also stipulate that this advice must be independent and unbiased by any financial rewards that might be offered to the professional.

More overtly ethical qualities stressed are those of non-discrimination, the maintenance of confidentiality and the importance of obtaining informed consent from clients or service-users. These issues are stressed throughout the whole of Professional Ethics and have acquired a large and comprehensive literature. However, when producing materials via the pragmatic approach, information regarding an appropriate interpretation of these terms can normally be found within the relevant code of practice or legislation. For example, the GMC offers advice on seeking patient's consent,[21] as does the British Dietetic Association.[22] Examples within legislation can be found in the Human Tissue Bill,[23] which includes definitions of what is meant by informed consent, while bodies such as the Scottish Executive provide a review of the literature relating to mental health legislation which includes coverage of capacity, competency and consent.[24] The ETHICS Project website also includes downloadable information on consent and confidentiality.

All links are available live at http://www.prs-ltsn.ac.uk/ethics

[21] http://www.gmc-uk.org/standards/CONSENT.HTM

[22] http://www.bda.uk.com/Downloads/informed%20consent.pdf

[23] http://www.parliament.the-stationery-office.co.uk/pa/cm200304/cmbills/009/04009.1-6.html#J028

[24] http://www.scotland.gov.uk/cru/kd01/purple/review20.htm

How do your students see Research Ethics Committees?

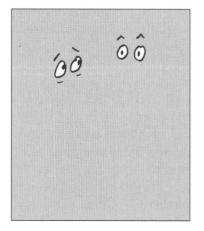

As a fog of obscurity...

... as an obstacle ...

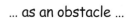

... or as the Inquisition

Research Ethics Committees (RECs)

Ethical scrutiny of research proposals is now many layered and evidence of ethical awareness is an integral part of a well-structured funding application. For example, the Wellcome Trust requires the following information and licenses for a funding application.

- Signed collaborators' forms from researchers willing to participate in or provide materials for the project.
- Ethical permission for studies involving patients and the use of material from human subjects (e.g. blood samples).
- Regulatory approval for research involving gene therapy from applicants' Local Research Ethics Committee, University's Genetic Manipulation Committee, Gene Therapy Advisory Committee and Medicines Control Agency.[25]
- For research using NHS facilities or patients, confirmation that the applicants are acting within the principles of the Statement of Partnership on Non-Commercial R&D in the NHS.
- Personal and project licences for any animal experiments that require Home Office approval.[26]

Other funding bodies show a clear concern for ethical standards. The BBSRC (Biotechnology and Biological Sciences Research Council) expects all grant holders to show that they are aware of the potential ethical implications of their work and research applications may be referred to its Advisory Group on BBSRC Response to Issues of Public Concern, a group which includes not only professionals but lay members who can provide '*viewpoints representative of the wider population*'.[27] PPARC (Particle Physics and Astronomy Research Council) requires that there must be,

reliable systems and processes in place for the prevention of scientific misconduct e.g. plagiarism, falsification of data, together with clearly defined arrangements for investigating and resolving allegations of scientific misconduct.[28]

The ESRC, which funds research addressing economic and social concerns states that it '*attaches considerable importance to the maintenance of high ethical standards in the research it supports*'[29]

All links are available live at http://www.prs-ltsn.ac.uk/ethics

[25] Medicines and Healthcare Products Regulatory Agency (Medicines Control Agency): http://www.mca.gov.uk/
[26] http://www.wellcome.ac.uk/en/1/biosfginflic.html
[27] http://www.bbsrc.ac.uk/society/research/resp_ethic.html
[28] http://home.pparc.ac.uk/rs/rgh/rghData.asp?sb=1.5&si=n
[29] Taken from the ESRC's web pages—http://www.esrc.ac.uk/esrccontent/ResearchFunding/sec22.asp

while the Medical Research Council publishes a number of downloadable documents as part of its Ethics Series, defining its concerns on ethical issues.[30]

Until recently Research Ethics Committee approval has applied mainly to postgraduate or professional researchers, but undergraduate projects are increasingly being treated to the same level of scrutiny as any other research work. Similarly, while audit projects do not currently need REC approval, many institutions have separate audit committees and are concerned that qualitative research is reviewed as rigorously as clinical research.

In general, it appears that all students in research oriented disciplines will benefit from some familiarity with the way RECs operate and the benchmarking statements reflect this. For example, the subject skills statement for Psychology requires that the student

[i]s aware of the ethical context of psychology as a discipline and can demonstrate this in relation to personal study, particularly with regard to the research project. [31]

Jane Pearson[32] a member of the North West Multi Centre Research Ethics Committee states that Research Ethics Committees have three primary functions:

1) To protect research subjects from harm
2) To facilitate good quality research
3) To protect researchers

In addition to the above, they also serve:

■ To enable researchers to obtain funding from grant bodies
■ To enable research to be published

When introducing students to ethics through a consideration of the application procedure for obtaining REC approval for a project, it is worth stressing that these regulations aim to protect researchers as well as research subjects. This point is also highlighted by Diane Beale's article (see p. 29) in which safeguards for researcher safety and welfare is a key concern of the Institute Ethics Committee. It is easy for students to see research ethics as a hurdle to be got over, rather than as a supportive framework, so a stress on the benefits to

---

All links are available live at http://www.prs-ltsn.ac.uk/ethics

[30] http://www.mrc.ac.uk/index/publications/publications-ethics_and_best_practice.htm
[31] http://www.qaa.ac.uk/crntwork/benchmark/phase2/psychology.pdf
[32] Pearson, J. (2003) Presentation on the Role of Research Ethics Committees, offered at ETHICS Project Workshop, King's Manor, York

them of REC scrutiny may be a useful way of encouraging a positive and constructive attitude.

Sources of information on RECs and their relevance to different kinds of research ethics are numerous, and mainly web-based due to the rapidly evolving nature of the framework. This guide cannot provide a comprehensive list of sources (and if it could the list would probably be obsolete by the time of publication) but the links specified in the next section will offer a guide for teachers needing material for an introduction to REC activity.

RECs in Higher Education

The most useful starting point will probably be the web pages of your own institution. Most colleges of Higher Education with active research programmes will have their own Research Ethics Committee and the more research intensive units will have several committees operating at department or centre level. For example:

- University College Chester—Centre for Public Health Research: **http://www.chester.ac.uk/cphr/resources.html**
- University of Cambridge—Human Biology Research Ethics Committee, Human Biology: **http://www.bio.cam.ac.uk/sbs/hbrec/**
- University of Sheffield—School of Health & Related Research: **http://www.shef.ac.uk/uni/academic/R-Z/scharr/resethics/**
- Queen's University Belfast—Psychology: **http://www.psych.qub.ac.uk/ethics/prec.html**

For external approval, the following outline indicates the basic structure at the time of writing.

Primary Sources

Many RECs refer ultimately to legislation on Human Rights. In the UK, this has its basis in the Human Rights Act 1998, an act designed to give further effect to rights and freedoms guaranteed under the European Convention on Human Rights.[33]

The government department with responsibility for ensuring the successful implementation of the Human Rights Act (1998) is the Department of Constitutional Affairs.[34]

Northern Ireland also has the Northern Ireland Human Rights Commission.[35]

All links are available live at http://www.prs-ltsn.ac.uk/ethics

[33] See **http://www.hmso.gov.uk/acts/acts1998/19980042.htm** for the Human Rights Act, **http://www.hri.org/docs/ECHR50.html** for the European Convention on Human Rights
[34] **http://www.dca.gov.uk/hract/hramenu.htm**
[35] **http://www.nihrc.org/**

For Medical Ethics, a primary source will be the *Declaration of Helsinki*, a statement by the World Medical Association designed to provide guidance to physicians and other participants in medical research on human subjects (including research on identifiable human material or identifiable data).[36]

With regard to animal experimentation, the Home Office provides information on the use of animals in scientific procedures. Of particular use to teachers is the section on Frequently Asked Questions which gives some insight into the ethical issues of public concern.[37]

Within the National Health Service, the Governance arrangements for NHS Research Ethics Committees (GAfREC) is the primary source. It draws on the Department of Health's Research Governance Framework for Health and Social Care, in which particular reference is made to:

the duties and accountability of all NHS organisations that agree to host any research, whether undertaken by its own employees or by others (GAfREC 1.2)

The primary concern in any research study is identified as:

the dignity, rights, safety and well-being of participants (GAfREC 1.3.)

With regard to the education and training of REC members and administrators, the regulations state that:

REC members have a need for initial and continuing education and training regarding research ethics, research methodology and research governance.

Appointing Authorities shall provide, within the annual budget for its REC(s), resources for such training, guidance on which will be issued by the Department of Health. (GAfREC 4.10/11)

In addition to the relevant expert members, at least one third of the membership of the REC should be made up of lay members, where lay member is defined as a member who is independent of the NHS, either as employee or in a non-executive role, and whose primary personal or professional interest is not in a research area (GAfREC 6.5). At least half of the "lay" members must be persons

---

All links are available live at http://www.prs-ltsn.ac.uk/ethics

[36] http://www.wma.net/e/policy/b3.htm

[37] See http://www.homeoffice.gov.uk/comrace/animals/ for further information.

who are not, and never have been, either health or social care professionals, and who have never been involved in carrying out research involving human participants, their tissue or data (GAfREC 6.7). The BBSRC's advisory group (mentioned above) has a similar lay component, while the British Medical Association's Medical Ethics Committee includes members drawn from law and moral philosophy. It is worth bearing this point in mind when preparing students to submit proposals to committees of this type, since the information supplied must be accessible, as far as possible, to people with no subject specific knowledge.[38]

LRECs and MRECs

Responsibility for reviewing research proposals to ensure that they meet GAfREC's stringent requirements is carried out within the NHS via Local Research Ethics committees (LRECs) overseen by regional Offices of Research Ethics Committees (ORECs). LRECs give permission for research carried out within the boundaries of a single research site, defined as the geographical area covered by one Health Authority.

Research carried out within the boundaries of five or more research sites requires Multi-Centre Research Ethics Committee (MREC) approval. For research undertaken within two, three or four research sites, researchers can choose whether to make applications to the LRECs for each site, or a single application to an MREC. [39]

This system is coordinated and managed by the Central Office for Research Ethics Committees or COREC. COREC provides useful information on its web pages, including downloadable forms.[40]

COREC also has a training section which provides help in putting together guides aimed at REC members and Administrators, but which could also be of use to teachers aiming to familiarise students with the way RECs function. There are plans to include additional information such as sample cases, a core syllabus and common issues facing RECs with the relevant ethical arguments.

Although this network exists principally to serve the needs of research involving patients, service-users and staff, its Research Ethics Committees may also provide an opinion on:

All links are available live at http://www.prs-ltsn.ac.uk/ethics

[38] http://www.dh.gov.uk/assetRoot/04/05/86/09/04058609.pdf

[39] These details were taken from the COREC website and apply to the end of February 2004. Please check the web pages for updated information.

[40] http://www.corec.org.uk/index.htm

ethics of similar research studies not involving the categories listed above, carried out for example by private sector companies, the Medical Research Council (or other public sector organisations), charities or universities. [41]

Scotland has its own MRECs and LRECs but Research ethics appraisal is ultimately the responsibility of the Chief Scientist Office of the Scottish Executive. The online resource "Scotland's Health on the Web" or SHOW offers information on ethical standards , including links to online versions of the Adults with Incapacity (Scotland) Act 2000 and the Confidentiality and Security Advisory Group for Scotland. [42]

Wales currently has one MREC and a number of LRECs. Details can be found via the web pages of the Wales Officer for Research and Development for Health and Social Care. [43]

An idea of the way LRECs work can be obtained by visiting a few sample websites:

- Cambridge: **http://www.addenbrookes.org.uk/serv/resethics/lrec1.html**
- North Cumbria: **http://www.northcumbriahealth.nhs.uk/lrec/**
- Dyfed Powys: **http://www.dyfpws-ha.wales.nhs.uk/ethics/**

A complete list of Local Research Ethics Committees can be found on the COREC website. [44]

All links are available live at http://www.prs-ltsn.ac.uk/ethics

[41] **http://www.corec.org.uk/whenToApply.htm**

[42] **http://www.show.scot.nhs.uk/cso/index.htm**

[43] **http://www.word.wales.gov.uk/content/ethics/index-e.htm**

[44] **http://www.corec.org.uk/index.htm**

Other Government Sources

The Health and Safety Executive (HSE) has a Research Ethics Committee responsible for

> the ethical conduct of studies which are designed to increase understanding of those workplace factors that contribute to occupational ill-health or give rise to decrements in performance which lead to an increased risk of accident. [45]

It reviews proposal with reference to the following criteria:

- Scientific validity
- Justifiability (potential benefits versus risk of harm)
- Non-maleficence
- Confidentiality and Privacy
- Informed Consent

The HSE's ethics webpage has details of the application procedure for REC approval, plus discussion papers and links to published guidelines.[46]

Many other bodies have their own RECs:

Hospitals

- The Royal Marsden:
  http://www.royalmarsden.org/research/ethics_committee.asp
- University Hospital, Birmingham:
  http://www.uhb.nhs.uk/about/research/ethics.htm
- Glasgow Royal Infirmary:
  http://www.ngt.org.uk/research/ethics/griethicscom.htm

Professional Organisations

- See the UK Clinical Ethics Network web pages for a list of health-related professional ethics bodies with ethics committees:
  http://www.ethics-network.org.uk/Committee/professional/professional.htm

Examples:

All links are available live at http://www.prs-ltsn.ac.uk/ethics

[45] http://www.hse.gov.uk/research/ethics/index.htm
[46] http://www.hse.gov.uk/research/ethics/index.htm

- The British Contact Lens Association:
  http://www.bcla.org.uk/guidelines.asp
- West Midlands Institute of Psychotherapy
  http://www.wmip.org/council.html

Private Sector Employers

- ADAS (Research based consultancy to rural and land-based industries): http://www.adas.co.uk/home/policy.html?topid=4#ethics

Other independent organisations

- Dr Foster (an online service which 'collects and analyses information on the availability and quality of health services in the   UK').
  See http://www.drfoster.co.uk/home/ethics.asp

Subject-Specific Approval

For some types of research, other types of approval may be required.

Embryo and Embryonic Stem Cell Research

The Human Fertilisation and Embryology Act, 1990[47] specifies that all human embryo research conducted in the UK must be licensed by the Human Fertilisation and Embryology Authority (HFEA). This act covers the creation and storage of embryos in addition to their actual use in research. Since 1991, when the act was amended to allow the use of embryos in stem cell research, the HFEA has also been the regulatory body for embryonic stem cell research in the UK. The HFEA's web pages provide information on:

- Accepted purposes for research of this type
- Current Research Projects licensed by the HFEA
- Research License application procedure

HFEA licenses are required in addition to the usual REC approval.[48]

Xenotransplantation

The United Kingdom Xenotransplantation Interim Regulatory Authority (UKXIRA)[49] was established in 1997 on the

---

All links are available live at http://www.prs-ltsn.ac.uk/ethics

[47] http://www.legislation.hmso.gov.uk/acts/acts1990/Ukpga_19900037_en_1.htm

[48] http://www.hfea.gov.uk/Research

[49] http://www.advisorybodies.doh.gov.uk/ukxira/

recommendation of the Advisory Group on the Ethics of Xenotransplantation, which was formed under the Chairmanship of Professor Ian Kennedy in 1995. It provides advice to the Secretaries of State for Health, Northern Ireland, Scotland and Wales on the actions needed to regulate xenotransplantation, including '*the acceptability of specific applications to proceed with xenotransplantation in humans.*'

The UKXIRA's website is a useful source of information on their background and terms of reference. There are downloadable versions of a range of publications in addition to a specific guidance on making proposals to conduct xenotransplantation on human subjects.[50]

Gene Therapy

Research involving somatic cell gene therapy (i.e. research on any cell other than sperm or egg cells) must be vetted by the Gene Therapy Advisory Committee (GTAC).[51] At the time of writing (February 2004), GTAC's holds that *all* gene therapy is classified as research, on the grounds that this procedure has not yet developed to the point where it can be considered as treatment. GTAC's terms of reference are:

- To consider and advise on the acceptability of proposals for gene therapy research on human subjects, on ethical grounds, taking account of the scientific merits of the proposals and the potential benefits and risks.
- To work with other agencies that have responsibilities in this field, including local research ethics committees, and agencies with statutory responsibilities—the Medicines Control Agency, the Health and Safety Executive and the Department of the Environment.
- To provide advice to United Kingdom Health Ministers on developments in gene therapy research and their implications.[52]

GTAC's website provides information on research applications, events and useful links, in addition to a range of downloadable publications and research.[53]

All links are available live at http://www.prs-ltsn.ac.uk/ethics

[50] http://www.advisorybodies.doh.gov.uk/ukxira/

[51] http://www.advisorybodies.doh.gov.uk/genetics/gtac/

[52] Taken from GTAC's website, http://www.advisorybodies.doh.gov.uk/genetics/gtac/

[53] http://www.advisorybodies.doh.gov.uk/genetics/gtac/

Common Themes

As with Professional codes, the same issues and principles recur across the network of RECs. There is also considerable consensus between RECs and Professional Codes of Conduct. For example, the ESRC identifies the following as *minimal* ethical standards:

- Honesty : to research staff and subjects about the purpose, methods and intended and possible uses of the research, and any risks involved.
- Confidentiality: of information supplied by research subjects and anonymity of respondents.
- Independence and impartiality: of researchers from the subject of the research.[54]

For research involving human subjects informed consent is also of key concern.

With regard to the use of animals, the Wellcome Trust states that it is

committed to the principles of reduction, replacement and refinement. [55]

Applying the principle of reduction means reducing the number of animals used to the minimum. The principle of replacement means that the researcher will replace live animals with tissues (derived from humans or animals) wherever possible. The principle of refinement involves amending the design of the experiment to obtain the maximum amount of information from the minimum number of animals (see the pragmatic Case Study at the end of this section for a further consideration of these principles).

Overall, despite the complex multi-layered nature of the REC network, it is possible to construct modules relevant to students at undergraduate, post-graduate and CPE level based around key ethical principles and themes.

All links are available live at http://www.prs-ltsn.ac.uk/ethics

[54] Taken from the ESRC's web pages—**http://www.esrc.ac.uk/esrccontent/ResearchFunding/sec22.asp**
[55] **http://www.wellcome.ac.uk/en/1/biosfginf.html**

Clinical Ethics—the Power and the Glory

Bryan Vernon
University of Newcastle

I have been asked to contribute this article as a Lecturer in Health Care Ethics and a member of a clinical ethics committee. The article demonstrates the ways in which an understanding of health care ethics has practical value in the real world of health service Trusts.

I was in the unusual position to choose my own job title when I was appointed. I deliberately selected the phrase 'Health Care Ethics' as, although the majority of my work involves teaching medical students, the phrase 'Medical Ethics' implies that the ethical dilemmas doctors face are of a different nature from those faced by other health care professionals. Similarly 'Nursing Ethics' implies that nurses face different dilemmas. I would argue that a nurse who disagrees with an order from a doctor is in a similar position to a registrar who disagrees with an order from the consultant. I think it is too simplistic to say that nurses care while doctors treat, as roles become increasingly blurred. The phrase 'Health Care Ethics' also allows for the ethical dilemmas faced by managers whom other health care professionals often glibly dismiss as acting from pure pragmatism.

When I chaired the Newcastle Mental Health NHS Trust in 1991 I formed the first Trust clinical ethics committee in the UK. This was followed by an ethics committee for one of the long-stay wards as staff grappled with issues raised by their move into the community. I am a member of an ethics committee of a local Trust for people with learning difficulties, a committee which meets infrequently, and of the Newcastle Hospitals Clinical Ethics Advisory Committee which meets about every six to eight weeks.

The Newcastle Hospitals Clinical Ethics Advisory Committee is chaired by an old age physician and comprises the Chair of the Trust who is a surgeon, a philosopher, a nurse philosopher, a social scientist and an ethicist. There are consultants in palliative care, child health, intensive care and old age psychiatry and a registrar in public health who chairs one of the LRECs as well as a nurse consultant in old age and a nursing professor. Members give the impression that their respect for one another goes beyond mere politeness and do not appear to have adopted entrenched positions.

The committee exists to assist in developing a defensible resolution of conflicting claims where there is no consensus about values in the provision of treatment or care in a Trust setting. Our role is one of clarifying facts, assumptions and the basis for the conflict and then testing possible solutions.

The definition of ethics that I value and frequently use comes from Al Jonsen, who wrote, 'Ethics is... the moral limitation placed on power. Thus the origins of medical ethics lie in the realization that the power of knowledge and skill brought to bear on the vulnerability of the sick can be used to exploit and dominate. The ethics of service nourished in western medicine goes beyond prohibiting the abuse of power and demands that power be dedicated to the strengthening of the weak.'[56]

The use of power merits exploration. As a committee we say that anyone has the power to refer cases to us. As yet the data is inconclusive as to whether they do. A common feature of the ethics committees I have been involved with is that there is an anxiety that there may be a flood of issues if too much energy is devoted to seeking them out, and no clear idea as to how many issues per year would be enough. What are the criteria here, and how can they be judged? There is scope for considerable research here. Are Trust employees concealing ethical issues that they would like to discuss? Would further education in Ethics uncover ethical issues that staff had not noticed?

There are issues of power within the committee. While there are people on the committee who are not employed by the Trust, they are sufficiently involved with the Health Service to be atypical—but who can represent patients in such a forum? There are more doctors than nurses, no hospital porters, cleaners or technicians. We may hope that any hierarchy is challenged by the anarchy of the marketplace of ideas. Ideas can emerge from many sources, and if they are good ones which involve sound reasons they deserve to be adopted no matter what their provenance. It is possible, though, that we are missing some insights because of a shared set of assumptions that we are too myopic to see.

I would suggest that there are four qualities required of members of Clinical ethics committees. The first is insight into ourselves and our own motivations. This will never be absolute, but may be adequate. An awareness of personal and group conflicts of interest is vital.

Secondly a member requires humility. There may be personal and professional kudos attached to membership of an ethics committee—the glory of the title of this piece—but we know that we rely on the insights of others whom we hold in mutual respect to prevent us from believing that we are God's gift to the Trusts we serve. A moment's reflection suggests that God might in fact have done better.

Thirdly we need a BS detector. The practice of ethics can encourage a certain preciousness among those who come within its orbit. We are probably all guilty of this at some point or another, but better at seeing it in others than in ourselves. A reader of this article may find examples that I have overlooked, and if so, I apologise.

Finally we require some skill in ethical analysis. It is quite legitimate for those who are not on the committee to question the authority of those who are. We are members because we are thought to possess some kind of ethical expertise, but this is an elusive quality. It is possible to demonstrate an ability to question assumptions, to weigh evidence and to evaluate arguments. While the process may be admirable, the outcome, as a decision, may be reached by entirely intuitive means.

The educational challenge is to develop people with insight who have the courage to ask difficult questions and who have the clarity of thinking to grasp what these questions are. We need to develop team players, as most ethical issues are in fact resolved as a result of good communication within teams, rather than in an ethics committee.

All links are available live at http://www.prs-ltsn.ac.uk/ethics

[56] Jonsen A.R. 'The end of medical ethics' *Journal of the American Geriatrics Society.* 1992:40;393-7

Ethics in Applied Research and Teaching

Diane Beale

Institute of Work, Health & Organisations, University of Nottingham

This paper discusses the management of the ethical implications of applied research and teaching, particularly in areas concerned with personal and sensitive issues. It considers particularly research, teaching and practice in occupational and health psychology, and related fields. It describes the role of an ethics committee in a postgraduate institute in applied psychology to illustrate how some of the issues might be addressed effectively to ensure ethical practice. It takes as a central premise that researchers and students should be encouraged to "think ethically" rather than simply apply a code or set of standards.

The Institute of Work, Health and Organisations carries out research in areas such as work-related stress, violence, bullying & harassment; positive emotions and behaviour at work; work-family conflict; selection and training evaluation; knowledge management; health and safety management, and risk assessment for psychosocial hazards; and management of chronic illness at work. Many of these areas involve highly sensitive issues for the participants and research is often carried out in co-operation with employing organisations.

The Institute provides research training for PhD students in all its areas of research. It also provides a variety of Masters courses in occupational and health psychology and their areas of overlap, as well as in more general research methods in psychology. Some courses are accredited to provide the basis for chartership of the British Psychological Society (BPS). Students come from a diverse range of cultures and nationalities. Part of the training is to assist students always to think carefully about the implications of their work.

The Ethics Committee

The Institute Ethics Committee was set up to oversee the application of ethics to the activities of the Institute. Its responsibilities include:

- to establish and follow procedures for evaluating ethical implications of Institute research projects;
- to agree standards based on the British Psychological Society (BPS) Code of Conduct;
- to ensure standards are met in all projects;
- to act as a point of contact for staff to discuss ethical issues arising from their research;
- to educate students regarding ethics in research;
- to ensure safeguards for researcher safety and welfare; and
- to require conformity to the University's Data Protection Policy.

30

The Ethics Committee requires an Ethics Submission to be completed for *all* research projects. This ensures that the implications of all Institute research has been thought through in terms of ethics as well as theory and methodology. The submission includes:

- a project description;
- an Ethics Submission Form comprising:
  - a checklist of ethical features of the study, and
  - details of these and measures to address them;
- materials, e.g. questionnaires, interview schedules, including
- wording of introductions and consent forms.

All submissions have to be approved by two members of academic or senior research staff who are not directly involved in the project. Any substantial changes to the research require further approval.

The Ethics Committee comprises core members, who deal with the regular ethics submissions from research-active staff, and act as a focus for discussion of ethical problems that emerge from research. It also involves all members of the Institute academic and research staff, plus PhD students, in a single dedicated meeting to assess all the MSc students' submissions for empirical research projects. As well as sharing out the burden of processing so many submissions, this exercise provides training for new researchers in identifying problematic ethical issues. The Committee also has a number of external members who are able to review procedures.

Ethical Codes of Conduct

The main ethical code that applies to this type of research in this country is the British Psychological Society (BPS) *Professional Code of Conduct, Ethical Principles and Guidelines* (2000). However, it is also instructive to take account of codes from other countries, such as the American Psychological Association (APA) *Ethics Code* (2002), and those covering allied disciplines, such as the World Medical Association *Declaration of Helsinki* (2002), in order to gain a wider appreciation of the issues.

The BPS Professional Code of Conduct covers issues of competence and conduct. It requires psychologists to maintain and develop their competence, and to recognise and work within the limits of that competence. It requires them to behave professionally, not damaging clients or undermining public confidence. It contains ethical principles for conducting research with human participants based on respect and consideration for those participants. These are particularly important in dealing with sensitive issues and traumatic experiences. Briefly, these principles include:

- Obtaining valid and informed consent from participants. This involves providing appropriate information to participants, and ensuring that they are both competent to give consent and free to give it voluntarily.
- Avoiding using deception, unless this is impossible because of the nature of the phenomenon under investigation.
- Providing adequate debriefing to complete participants' understanding of the research, particularly where deception has been necessary or negative emotions might have been generated.

- Allowing participants to withdraw from the research either during the procedure or subsequently, and allowing them to withdraw their consent for their contribution to be used.
- Establishing and maintaining appropriate confidentiality.
- Protecting participants from physical/psychological harm in procedures, and from exacerbating any pre-existing conditions.
- Preserving privacy in observational research.
- Ensuring that colleagues observe ethical principles.

The APA *Ethics Code* (2002) advocates five general principles, which are "aspirational in nature. Their intent is to guide and inspire psychologists toward the very highest ethical ideals of the profession." The principles indicate the wide-ranging responsibilities for psychologists to apply in research and practice. They are entitled "beneficence and nonmaleficence", "fidelity and responsibility", "integrity", "justice" and "respect for people's rights and dignity".

The World Medical Association *Declaration of Helsinki* (2002, para. 5) also provides the concept of putting the welfare of the individual participant before the good of society. "In medical research on human subjects, considerations related to the well-being of the human subject should take precedence over the interests of science and society." This principle often comes into play in deciding the competing interests of sponsoring organisations and individual employees in applied research, as discussed in the next section.

Ethical Responsibilities in Research

Most codes of ethical conduct concentrate on the responsibilities of researchers towards the participants, or subjects, of the research. They also deal briefly with responsibilities to other members of the profession and to society as a whole. However, for truly ethical research, there are wider and deeper implications that should be taken into account. Researchers should recognise responsibilities to:

- Participants in the research;
- Sponsoring and host organisations, if applicable;
- Themselves, as individuals;
- Their colleagues; and
- Their own organisations, including their academic institution, employer and professional body.

One of the key dilemmas that is ever present when working with organisations is balancing the requirements of, and responsibility to, the host organisation with responsibilities towards the employees who participate in the research. In particular, both parties have to be given realistic expectations about confidentiality. Reports back to the management have to protect the identity of participants as far as is reasonable without undermining the value of the research, which the organisation may have paid for in the first place. Participants should be informed of the safeguards put in place to protect their anonymity or, if anonymity cannot be guaranteed, they should be made aware that their identity may be apparent in reports.

Further responsibilities come into play with regard to organisations. There is an obligation to provide useful feedback to a host organisation whether or not it has commissioned the research. Further, any recommendations made must take into account the implications for the organisation, should be realistic and based on sound evidence, with the limitations of the research properly explained. An associated responsibility concerns the publication of research, where confidentiality should apply to host organisations as well as participants. Specific permission should be obtained from an organisation to identify it in any publication.

Researcher Safety and Well-being

One aspect of ethical research that has rarely been mentioned in ethics literature is the welfare of the researchers themselves. In particular, the safety of research assistants and students in collecting data is rarely considered, except in terms of specific laboratory safety procedures, or similar. Paterson, Gregory and Thorne (1999), as a notable exception, have attempted to address aspects of this problem by designing a protocol for researcher safety in field research. However, a more complete consideration encompasses not only physical safety but also psychological well-being and personal reputation.

Physical safety relates to risk from accident, illness or violence. These might occur in relation to a number of situations in applied research including travel, lone and night working, and the inherently dangerous working conditions within some industries. It is incumbent on research supervisors to ensure that there are adequate personal safety measures included in arrangements for data collection. These might include, for example, researchers notifying a colleague of their whereabouts, time of return, a contact number, and what to do if they do not return at the time expected. Night working might require working in pairs or, at least, provision of safe transport. Working in a number of industries might involve exposure to dangerous situations where training in, and adherence to, organisational safety procedures is vital. It is important that such training, any necessary supervision and insurance issues are negotiated with the host organisation at the beginning of a project.

Risks to psychological well-being might come from such things as exposure to distressing information. Work-related violence, and health and safety management are obvious research areas that may require researchers to view disturbing reports or CCTV footage, or to conduct interviews with victims of traumatic incidents. It is important that safeguards are in place to ensure that researchers are not adversely affected by such exposure and have regular opportunities for debriefing and discussion. Equally, supervisors should ensure that researchers are not placed in situations where they are vulnerable to harassment or intimidation, for example a female researcher going into an unknown all-male environment, or vice versa. Conversely, they should be careful not to put themselves into situations that might compromise their reputation or be open to misinterpretation as being illegal.

Data Protection

A final area that can be included in the scope of ethical working comprises data protection issues, largely because of links with confidentiality and consent. Most organisations now have a code of practice with which researchers should comply. In line with legal requirements these pertain to:

- Obtaining data, i.e. ensuring that only data in which there is a legitimate research interest is collected, and ensuring that participants have given consent having had information about use and storage of the data;
- Processing and securely storing the data, whether hardcopy or electronic;
- Disclosing the information only to individuals and in circumstances agreed by the participants;
- Deleting or archiving information, again in circumstances agreed by the participants, after a given period or for a given reason.

These guidelines require researchers to have respect for the information supplied by participants and to be scrupulous in the use that is made of this information.

Ethics in Teaching

In the teaching of ethics the Institute staff aim to develop an appreciation of ethical issues in applied psychological research, increase awareness of relevant ethical codes of conduct, and provide practical experience of preparing a submission to an ethics committee. Further than that, they aim to encourage students to "think ethically" rather than simply adhere to a set of rules or guidelines. This involves thinking through any intended research and considering what effect it might have on the participants, any organisations involved and others parties. In addition, they aim to increase awareness of researcher safety and data protection issues.

These aims are achieved both via specific lectures and workshops, and by incorporating ethical considerations into all teaching. All taught courses include an early lecture in the basic methods and philosophy module. More detailed consideration is given in a lecture in the professional and ethical issues module, including group work examining a range of research scenarios. Specific ethical issues are included in teaching for particular subject areas, for example for selection. In addition, Masters students complete an empirical project for which they have to complete and submit an Ethics Committee submission, following a practical workshop. For research students there are also Institute Research Days, which regularly include workshops and discussions on particular ethical issues that have emerged in the course of Institute research projects.

Conclusion

In conclusion, the Ethics Committee sees its role as keeping all researchers alert to ethical issues in order to protect against inadvertent risks to participants, researchers and associated organisations. It promotes high ethical standards from all and teaches good practice to novice researchers. To achieve this effectively, it attempts to keep abreast of developments in practice, law etc. and to ensure that new issues are debated and consensus reached.

References

American Psychological Association (APA) *Ethics Code* (2002). Retrieved December 6, 2003, **http://www.apa.org/ethics/**

British Psychological Society (BPS) Professional Code of Conduct, Ethical Principles and Guidelines (2000). Leicester: BPS. Retrieved December 6, 2003, **http://www.bps.org.uk/about/rules5.cfm**

Paterson, B. L., Gregory, D., & Thorne, S. (1999). A protocol for researcher safety. Qualitative Health Research, 9(2), 259-269.

World Medical Association Declaration of Helsinki (2002). Retrieved December 6, 2003, **http://www.wma.net/e/policy/b3.htm**

A Case Study

Scenario

Extract from a Research Proposal designed to test the effects of exposure to fertiliser XYZ™ on kidney function.

Experimental Subjects: 100 healthy, six week old rats. Mixed sex. Approved supplier.

Maintenance: The rats will be housed in individual plastic tanks with food and water available 24/7 in the University's purpose built facility. They will be cared for and monitored round the clock by trained and experienced staff.

Palliative Care: Previous studies (Smith *et al.* (1999) suggest that rats exposed to higher levels of XYZ™ may develop minor skin lesions over the last four or five weeks. Topical analgesia will be administered to minimise discomfort.

Experimental Procedure: The rats will be divided randomly into 4 groups of 25 and exposed to varying levels of XYZ™ administered in their drinking water.

> Group 1—Control (no exposure to XYZ™)
> Group 2—Exposed to 10 parts per million of XYZ™
> Group 3—Exposed to 100 parts per million of XYZ™
> Group 4—Exposed to 1000 parts per million of XYZ™

At the end of the 3 month exposure period the rats will be despatched humanely and their kidneys removed for microscopic and biochemical analysis.

Ethical Issues

This scenario is designed primarily to help the students understand the principles of reduction, replacement and refinement. This would mean asking three key questions:

1) Reduction: Could a comparable experimental outcome have been achieved using fewer rats?
2) Replacement: Could a comparable experimental outcome have been achieved using a cultured kidney tissue cell line rather than live animals?
3) Refinement: If the use of live animals is appropriate, does the experiment maximise the amount of information that could be obtained from their use. Could the experiment be modified in order to produce more/better results without increasing the number of animals or causing them additional distress?

Using the Case Study with Students

Students might gain additional credit for noting the reference to previous studies, and asking whether the proposal is merely duplicating work carried out elsewhere. They would be expected to show an awareness that refinement might sometimes indicate using more animals, because if the numbers proposed are too few to generate statistically significant results then those few rats will have been sacrificed needlessly. An introduction to the principles of reduction, replacement and refinement can be provided by the extract alone. In these circumstances students would be asked only to:

- recognise the relevance of the principles to the proposal;
- indicate which parts of the proposal would give cause for concern;
- indicate the questions that would be asked;
- suggest the kinds of additional information that might have been provided by the research applicant to show an awareness of the principles of reduction, replacement and refinement.

In the absence of more information about the research, they would not be able to evaluate whether the research met the requirements of these principles.

However, for more experienced students, the extract could be expanded to provide a fully defined dummy research proposal, with all the relevant scientific background, procedures *etc.* filled in. Students can then be invited to review the proposal as if they were a REC member, evaluating whether the research does actually fulfil the relevant ethical criteria. This would be a more demanding task and would also be time consuming, but can be a useful format for group work.

Embedded

Introduction

The embedded approach presents ethical issues within the context of some broader programme through which students explore what it means to be a 'professional' or to be Fit for Practice. In contrast to the pragmatic and theoretical approaches, it is possible to teach ethics via the embedded approach without ever mentioning the words 'ethical' or 'moral'. Students study ethics indirectly, by considering an area of professional interest which has a significant ethical dimension but which is not confined to it. However, students might still be asked to abstract the 'ethical' and subject it to scrutiny, for the embedded approach does not preclude encouraging some level of overt awareness of ethics. The 'embeddedness' of the title refers principally to the student's 'way in' to the subject; the context in which they first begin to think about the ethical aspects of their performance. There is no reason why they should not go on to explore more 'pragmatic' or 'theoretical' avenues but it worth noting that this does not always happen in practice, so that for some students ethics in Higher Education is an essentially embedded topic.

Ethics learning and teaching can be embedded in terms of its objectives and/or its mode of delivery.

The discussion will consider two forms of embeddedness with respect to learning and teaching objectives. The first presents ethics as a dimension of what it means to be a Professional; a conception that places as much emphasis on team-working as on subject-specific knowledge and skills. The second form predominates in medicine health and social care, and presents ethics as a component of Fitness for Practice; a conception that defines ethical obligations in relation to a general Duty of Care.

There will also be a consideration of three embedded ways in which ethics learning and teaching can be delivered, namely through Reflective Practice, Drama and Narrative. The last of these modes of delivery will be addressed in more detail by a guest contribution from Deborah Bowman Senior Lecturer in Medical Ethics and Law at St George's Hospital Medical School, University of London, in a paper that,

> considers the use of humanities as one imaginative device for facilitating learning in healthcare ethics and argues that narrative and emotion are powerful tools for engaging teachers and learners alike.

The final part of this section will present a case study using an example of an embedded teaching method: narrative.

Professionalism and Interprofessionalism

Benchmarking statements and professional codes of conduct indicate that Professional Ethics are now seen as an integral part of a graduate's ability to function effectively in the workplace. As a result, ethics may be embedded in the rapidly evolving notion of what it means to be a Professional, an ideal that links ethical behaviour to interpersonal communication, professional competence and management skills rather than a facility with moral theory.

For example, the General Medical Council's Duties of a Doctor[57] include the following:

- Treat every patient politely and considerately

- Recognise the limits of your professional competence

- Be honest and trustworthy

- Respect and protect confidential information

- Make sure that your personal beliefs do not prejudice your patients' care

- Act quickly to protect patients from risk if you have good reason to believe that you or a colleague may not be fit to practise.

By substituting the appropriate alternative to 'patient', any or all of these duties would be applicable to any profession. Though all have some ethically significant content, they go beyond moral concerns, and serve the general aim of maintaining public confidence and professional reputation.

Most of these duties have already been noted in the preceding discussion of the Pragmatic approach. This serves to highlight that it is not learning and teaching content that is at issue here, but the way in which it is presented. In the pragmatic approach students learn about honesty, non-discrimination, competence *etc.* as part of a code of practice that will be enforced by professional (and in many cases legal) sanctions. In the embedded approach, they address these themes by developing a sense of professional identity and a consequent way of working which is imbued by desirable ethical professional values and behaviours.

One important difference between the pragmatic and embedded approaches to professionalism is that while the former sees

---

All links are available live at http://www.prs-ltsn.ac.uk/ethics

[57] http://www.gmc-uk.org/standards/default.htm

regulation and the raising of standards as (in the first instance, at least) a set of externally imposed constraints, the embedded approach has a greater emphasis on personal autonomy. Ethics embedded in the notion of Professionalism or Fitness to Practice mandates that the individual takes responsibility for improving their own performance via a self-directed process of continuing professional development throughout their working lives. For example, the *Duties of a Doctor* include keeping their professional knowledge and skills up to date, [58] while The International Confederation of Midwives (ICM) states that midwives should;

> actively seek personal, intellectual and professional growth throughout their midwifery career, integrating this growth into their practice. [59]

The ICM requirement quoted above emphasises the holistic notion of the professional which is at issue here. This holism will find its counterpart in the concept of the service- user discussed in the following section on Fitness for Practice, and will also be seen to be reflected in the methods of delivery most often associated with the embedded approach. Rather than abstracting ethically significant behaviours from their broader context, the embedded approach leaves them *in situ*, encouraging students to acquire professional behaviour patterns which serve a number of ends simultaneously and, wherever possible, synergistically. An important part of this involves acquiring the ability to work with others, so that ethics embedded in the notion of professionalism, is further embedded in the notion of interprofessionalism.

Interprofessionalism is of growing importance in contexts such as scientific research and product development. For example, the benchmark statement on engineering states that:

All links are available live at http://www.prs-ltsn.ac.uk/ethics

[58] http://www.gmc-uk.org/standards/default.htm
[59] http://www.internationalmidwives.org/

> Engineers frequently work in multidisciplinary teams and need to understand the relationship of their work to that of other specialists and to be able to communicate with them. The essential features of this include communication and interpersonal skills, accountability, professional ethics and organisational management, all of which are expected to be refined and developed in the person's career.[60]

Here we have ethics embedded in the notion of an interprofessional worker for whom ethics is not a separate skill or a defined way of thinking but merely one aspect of collaborative working practice.

Health and social care in particular have been subject to increasing political pressure to deliver integrated services. [61] Malin *et al.* noted that Labour government policy requires a much closer harmonization across the primary health/social care boundary.

> With the present government placing great emphasis on collaboration, professionals skilled at working across organizational boundaries are in high demand. [62]

As might be expected, the ability to '*work with colleagues in the ways that best serve patients' interests*'[63] is a key requirement within the medical profession.

Even where service provision relies on nominally independent professionals there is pressure for collaboration to secure public welfare. For example, the Royal College of Veterinary Surgeons recognises the links between animal and child abuse and offers advice and support to members on balancing the conflicting claims of client confidentiality and the obligation to report cases of suspected child abuse. [64]

There are signs that Higher Education is already beginning to recognise the advantages of incorporating multidisciplinary education and training provision into their pre-registration programmes. For example, the Dundee University School of Nursing Mission Statement includes a commitment to '*encourage further development of multi-professional learning between medical, nursing and*

All links are available live at http://www.prs-ltsn.ac.uk/ethics

[60] **http://www.qaa.ac.uk/crntwork/benchmark/engineering.pdf**, p.6.

[61] NHS Executive, 1998; Department for Health and Personal Social Services, 1998; Scottish Office Department of Health, 1999; Welsh Office, 1998)

[62] Malin N. A, Wilmot S, & Beswick J. A. (2000) 'The use of an ethical advisory group in a learning disability service', *Journal of Learning Disabilities*, Vol. 4(2), 105-114, 2000 (10)

[63] **http://www.gmc-uk.org/standards/default.htm**

[64] **http://www.rcvs.org.uk/vet_surgeons/pdf/advice/animabuse_Mar03.pdf**

midwifery students and social work.'[65] The LTSN subject centre for Health Sciences and Practice recently commissioned a review to '*help teachers engage effectively in interprofessional education*'.[66] The use of interdisciplinary learning as a means towards the end of greater interprofessional cooperation is not, in itself, limited to ethical concerns but the Peach Report[67] concluded that the subjects seen to offer most scope for shared learning were ethics and communications skills. [68]

In more general terms, interdisciplinary classes can be used to facilitate mutual respect and understanding between the professions.[69] The more closely teaching and learning opportunities mimic real working conditions, the more effectively they prepare students to meet the challenges they will face in their chosen sphere. The ability to arrive at a morally defensible course of action in concert with co-workers from other professions is an essential component of this preparation and interdisciplinary groups can contribute by enabling students to understand the diversity of moral opinion, and the ways in which consensus can be reached in a complex and fluid working environment.

Fitness for Practice

Courses in Higher Education normally lead to the award of certificates, diplomas and degrees in recognition of the student's achievement of a given level of academic achievement but for subjects such as medicine, nursing, pharmacy, dentistry, social work and education, graduation will normally lead directly or indirectly to registration This means graduates in these disciplines must meet behavioural standards in addition to academic criteria to ensure their Fitness to Practice.

Fitness for Practice will normally include the duties specified in the preceding section on Professionalism and Interprofessionalism, but in service professions these duties are extended to define the general Duty of Care that these service-providers have towards their service-users.

The GMC's definition of the Duties of a Doctor emphasise the importance of showing respect for the patient's dignity and privacy, and also reflects the move towards greater client-centredness

---

All links are available live at http://www.prs-ltsn.ac.uk/ethics

[65] http://www.prs-ltsn.leeds.ac.uk/ethics/event.html

[66] LTSN Centre for Health Sciences & Practice (2002) *Interprofessional Education: Today, Yesterday and Tomorrow: A Review*, London: LTSN

[67] Peach L. (Chair) (1999) Fitness for Practice, Commissioned by The United Kingdom Central Council (UKCC) for Nursing, Midwifery and Health Visiting,
http://www.nmc-uk.org/cms/content/Publications/Fitness%20for%20practice.pdf

[68] *Ibid.* Para. 5.39.

[69] *Ibid.*

evidenced throughout health and social care. The doctor has a duty to:

- respect the rights of patients to be fully involved in decisions about their care;
- listen to patients and respect their views;
- give patients information in a way they can understand;
- make the care of your patient your first concern.

The conception of the client on which Fitness for Practice is based is an increasingly holistic one. For example, midwives are required to:

be able to analyse human occupation from an holistic perspective and the demands made on individuals in order to engage in occupations[70]

Similarly, radiographers must:

understand the need to respect, and so far as possible uphold, the rights, dignity and autonomy of every patient including their role in the diagnostic and therapeutic process.[71]

A key objective in promoting client-centredness is to empower them. For example, within social work, Barnes and Hugman argue that:

The positive effect of social work responses to contemporary social theory can be seen in the move away from a 'problem' focus to a 'growth/strength' focus, with intervention essentially controlled by the 'client'.[72]

Registrant occupational therapists must be aware of the:

evolution of the profession towards the current emphasis on autonomy and empowerment of individuals, groups and communities[73]

All links are available live at http://www.prs-ltsn.ac.uk/ethics

[70] http://www.internationalmidwives.org/

[71] http://www.hpc-uk.org/publications/standards_of_proficiency_ra.htm

[72] Barnes D.; Hugman R. 'Portrait of social work', *Journal of Interprofessional Care*, Vol. 16, no. 3, pp. 277-288

while midwives support:

empowering women to speak for themselves on issues affecting the health of women and their families in their culture/society.[74]

Finally, confidentiality, while present in the broader notion of professional behaviour, is central to the notion of Fitness to Practice, and is defined in the context of a relationship of trust between service-provider and service-user, in which the provider's responsibilities are oriented towards the needs of the service-user. Gastmans gives the following examples of patient-oriented responsibilities:

- Entering into a confidential relationship with the patient.

- Providing comfort and preserving human dignity in the face of pain and extreme breakdown.

- Presencing (being with a patient); providing comfort and communication through touch.

- Guiding patients through developmental and emotional changes.

- Helping patients to cope with the lifestyle consequences of their illness.

- Interpreting the illness by allowing patients themselves to verbalize and understand.[75]

Professionalism and Fitness for Practice define ethics in strongly relational terms, but where the former concentrates on interactions with other professionals, Fitness for Practice is centred on interactions between professional and service-user as mediated through an overarching Duty of Care. Ethical considerations will be a vital part of this duty of care, but ethics embedded in the notion of Fitness to Practice is seen as an integral part of a broader behaviour and skills set and cannot be abstracted without changing its nature.

The theoretical approach considered later in this guide p. 65 often concentrates on what Seedhouse terms specific or 'dramatic ethics' such as end of life issues and the domain of the tragic choice.[76]

[73] http://www.hpc-uk.org/publications/standards/Standards_of_Proficiency_Occupational_Therapists.pdf
[74] http://www.internationalmidwives.org/
[75] Gastmans, C. (1998) 'Challenges to Nursing Values in a Changing Nursing Environment', Nursing Ethics, Vol. 5. no. 3, pp. pp. 236-245
[76] Seedhouse D. (1998) Ethics: The Heart of Health Care, John Wiley & Sons: Chichester, p.39

However, much of Fitness for Practice is concerned with what Seedhouse calls "persisting ethics"; the underlying ethical issues that underpin daily working practice. Ashcroft argues that '*[m]edical ethical problems ... must be identified as features of an evolving medical Scenario*'.[77] These scenarios will involve a multiplicity of factors, only some of which will be morally significant and good ethical judgement will often be a way of acting rather than an interval of reflection and analysis. The professional must respond speedily, assessing the situation and "seeing" how they should proceed without being aware of any deliberative procedure. Accordingly, their training must help them to reach a point where their knowledge and understanding is so firmly embedded that correct decision-making is a rapid and seamless process resulting in actions that feel like second nature.

The following section will consider some teaching methods through which this somewhat ambitious learning and teaching objective might be pursued.

Note: In addition to the professional codes cited above, a detailed review of Fitness for Practice as it applies to nursing and midwifery can be found in the Peach report.[78]

All links are available live at http://www.prs-ltsn.ac.uk/ethics

[77] Ashcroft R.E. (2000) 'Teaching for Patient-Centred Ethics', in *Medicine, Health Care and Philosophy* 3: pp. 287–295
[78] http://www.nmc-uk.org/cms/content/Publications/Fitness%20for%20practice.pdf
Peach L. (Chair) (1999) *Fitness for Practice*, Commissioned by The United Kingdom Central Council (UKCC) for Nursing, Midwifery and Health Visiting

Methods

A common theme to emerge from discussion at the ETHICS Project workshops was the importance of demystifying ethics for both teachers and students. For many, this meant an avoidance of deep theory in favour of teaching via role-play, practice-based learning, narrative and other methods designed to help students engage in the moral issues as real challenges that they can expect to face in their working lives.

In some courses it may be possible to embed ethics learning and teaching in pre-existing modules, so that from the students' point of view it becomes almost invisible. For example, Ashcroft notes that in medical ethics,

> most assessments can be done as elements of assessment in, say, pediatrics, and in the form of clinical problem-solving exercises (often with actors or real patients).[79]

There are many embedded teaching methods in use, and the variety is likely to increase as teachers look for new ways to make ethics accessible to students from a variety of backgrounds, but for the purposes of this guide, three methods will be considered in a little more detail to give some idea of how the approach works in practice. What they all have in common is that they present ethics embedded within a complex situation that acts on students at many levels: rational/emotional, personal/professional, objective/subjective, conscious/subconscious. Morally significant decisions taken within this context are similarly embedded, with agents making choices in which they must weigh up such things as the practical effectiveness of the courses of action available to them, their competence to pursue those courses of action, the risks (to the service-user, themselves and others) and the dynamics of their relationship with the service-user (both social and emotional) in addition to evaluating it against ethical criteria, often in circumstances that require that decision to be made in a matter of moments.

All links are available live at http://www.prs-ltsn.ac.uk/ethics

[79] Ashcroft, R.E. (2000) 'Teaching for patient-centred ethics', *Medicine, Health Care and Philosophy* Vol. 3: pp. 287–295

i. Reflective Practice

Reflective practice involves students taking a 'deep' approach[80,81] to learning by reflecting on what they have learned within the context of their whole life's experience. They do this in order to:

- Better understand their own approach to learning.
- Consider how they might build and improve upon it.

Fitness for Practice requires life-long self-directed learning and Reflective Practice meets these criteria as it allows practitioners to develop techniques that can be readily incorporated into their own *modus operandi*.

Within medicine and healthcare, the concept of reflective processes in education has become increasingly valued as a means of enabling students to analyse their learning experiences in order to gain a new understanding and insight. Reflective practice assists in the integration of theory with practice and this helps students to improve their clinical reasoning skills. In nursing and psychology, reflective practice is a key activity in continuing professional development[82,83].

Learning outcomes from a successful application of reflective practice include:

- Learning to think critically about the learning process
- Learning to think creatively and innovatively about one's own performance
- Learning to implement those innovations and transform one's own practice (and through example, that of others).

All links are available live at http://www.prs-ltsn.ac.uk/ethics

[80] Ramsden, P. (1992), *Learning to Teach in Higher Education*, Routledge

[81] Entwistle, N., S. Thompson and H. Tait (1992). *Guidelines for Promoting Effective Learning in Higher Education*. Edinburgh: Centre for Research on Learning and Instruction

[82] Peach L. (1999), op. cit. Section 4.23

[83] The British Psychological Society, Division of Clinical Psychology: Policy Guidelines on Supervision in the practice of Clinical Psychology: http://www.bps.org.uk/documents/DCP_SupervisionGuidelines.pdf

The first of these, acquiring a critical approach to the learning process itself, can be of particular utility in professional ethics where teachers may feel that they are on as steep a learning curve as their students. Central to reflective practice is:

the ability to recognise and understand one's underlying assumptions about the meaning of teaching and learning in the subject and one's habitual responses to teaching situations, and the ability to interrogate the relationships between these. [84]

Teachers do not always attain the levels of self-awareness in relation to their teaching that they recommend to students as learners. However if students become skilled in reflective practice this helps to generate a constructive and collaborative learning environment in which the student is an equal partner in the learning process rather than a passive or subordinate recipient of the teacher's expertise. In this atmosphere, teacher and student may hope to learn from one another, and to improve their performance as exponents and practitioners of their subject and as self-learners; a synergy which is of great benefit in a contested and rapidly evolving subject such as professional ethics.

Teaching and learning resources on the use of reflective practice can be found on a number of LTSN websites (see the end of this section for details). Although the subject areas vary, it will be seen that the process of reflective practice is broadly similar across disciplines and can be applied directly to the teaching of ethics.

Reflection requires attention to:

- Description and Observation
- Self-awareness
- Diversity of culture—this is important as people are used to different forms of reflection
- Analysis and interpretation
- Planning[85]

There are many ways in which students can reflect on their performance, varying from reflective essays, presentations, group discussion, feedback from teachers/facilitators/mentors and self-evaluation to more complex outputs such as the preparation of a learning portfolio.

All links are available live at http://www.prs-ltsn.ac.uk/ethics

[84] http://hca.ltsn.ac.uk/resources/guides/refl_praca.php
[85] http://www.lancs.ac.uk/palatine/report-reflective-practice.htm

The advantages of this learning and teaching method for professional ethics lie in the extent to which it involves the student in their own education, both during and after Higher Education

It is a matter for discrimination and judgement how far the student should be encouraged to give overt and conscious attention to the moral implications of their behaviour, or whether they should judge their performance against some broader notion which has ethical values embedded in it.

Web based sources on the use of Reflective Practice:

- UK Centre for Legal Education (LTSN Subject Centre for Law): **http://www.ukcle.ac.uk/resources/reflection/**
- Palatine (LTSN Subject Centre for the performing arts): **http://www.lancs.ac.uk/palatine/report-reflective-practice.htm**
- Subject Centre for History: **http://hca.ltsn.ac.uk/resources/guides/refl_praca.php**

Further Reading on Reflective Practice:

- Schon, D. (1983) *Educating the Reflective Practitioner: How Professionals Think in Action,* London: Temple Smith
- Moon, J. (2001) *Reflections in Learning and Professional Practice: Theory and Practice,* London: Kogan Page

ii. Drama

Live drama can offer an exciting and energising way of presenting embedded ethical issues. It can be utilised in two ways within the embedded approach, dependent on whether students observe as an 'audience' or alternatively, take an active part in the role-play.

Use of Actors

In this format, the actors are not themselves involved in the learning process (at least in so far as professional ethics are concerned). The use of real people, present in person, helps to engage students' attention and arouse their concern. The actor(s) may speak directly to the 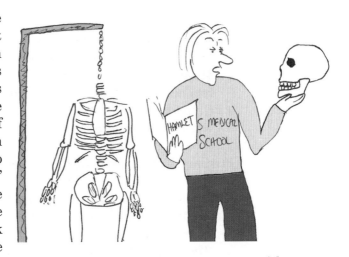 audience, as for example, a patient describing an encounter with a doctor, thus creating a direct relationship between their character and the students. If done effectively, this can produce a high level of engagement in the students, both intellectually and emotionally.

The students need not be confined to an entirely passive role; they can become participants in the drama by being invited to pose questions that the actor will then respond to in character ('respond' is used here in the dramatic senses of the word and should not be taken to indicate that the character will answer the question constructively or even at all). As this format requires the actor to go beyond the pre-prepared material the success of actor/student dialogue will depend heavily on the actor being given adequate preparation before the class, both in terms of the factual content of their character's situation and the character itself. In some cases, a real service-user or client can be asked to present a role of which they have some personal experience. This gives them a stronger basis on which to improvise answers to unscripted questions, but preparation is equally important to ensure that they are not distressed by the questioning process.

The need for improvisation can be avoided if the actors work entirely from a script. While this means that students will remain more passive with respect to the drama, they can still be drawn into a more active role by asking them to discuss and report on their reactions to what they have seen. An external perspective can be introduced by asking the actors to join in the discussion, but this time as themselves, drawing on their experience of playing the character and contrasting it with how they themselves might have felt in the same situation.

Another alternative for dramas that depict a professional making a morally significant choice is for the scene to be written with a number of alternative outcomes, dependent on the choice made. Students can be invited to view the drama up to the moment of decision before be asked to state which option the professional should take, either individually or following group discussion. The actors then return to play out the appropriate ending so that students can view and consider the projected outcome of their choice.

The use of actors can be expensive although there are resources available that can be accessed (see the end of this section for details). Another alternative for institutions that have schools of drama or student theatre groups is to involve students external to the ethics module in acting roles.

One advantage to performance-based ethics teaching is that it can be readily adapted to lecture-based formats, where classes must be offered to large numbers of students at a time, and without the opportunity to prepare the students via seminar or other forms of small-group work.

Performances can also be videoed and reused for subsequent classes. This will be of particular benefit in allowing students to draw on and evolve their interpretation of the performance in subsequent classes. Recorded material can also be used as the primary mode of delivery although this may result in a lesser level of engagement.

Use of Student Role-Play

If the students act the parts from themselves, role-play can become an integral part of the learning process. There are many scenarios that can be deployed here—mock trials, professional/service-user interactions, product-development teams and public debates being but a few. Role-play can be particularly effective if students are allocated roles that diverge from their own personality, so an important decision to be made when formulating teaching materials of this type is how roles will be allocated and whether every student will be required to take a role.

Most of the same options that were discussed in the preceding section on the use of actors will have some application here too, but with the additional possibility of having no audience at all for the final performance (it might be appropriate for the teacher/facilitator to take a participatory role).

There need be no script for role-play of this type. Rather, students are provided with information about their character's situation and personality on the basis of which they are asked to improvise. This information can be detailed, or can take the form of an outline that students must research and fill in for themselves.

Performances may be videotaped to facilitate discussion, feedback and evaluation (be it self-evaluation, peer evaluation, or evaluation by teacher/facilitator/external evaluator) but it should be born in mind that this can make the experience more stressful for some students. If there is an intention to use the recording as a future learning and teaching resource, consent should be sought from the students involved in the performance.

In addition to opportunities for role-play, the use of drama can be extended by inviting students to contribute to the writing of the script. This offers students who are uncomfortable with the idea of 'performing' to make a contribution, in addition to broadening the potential of the format as a learning and teaching device.

Outcomes

Whether the mode of delivery uses actors or student role-play, drama can be used to enrich students' perceptions of morally significant situations by helping them to:

- Think from multiple perspectives with regard to culture, gender, religion *etc.*
- Understand the service-user's point of view
- Empathise with others, even those with characters divergent from their own
- Promote a holistic view of professionals and service-users
- Comprehend what it feels like to make decisions under pressure and in sub-optimal conditions

Resources

Psci-coma guide to Internet resources on public engagement with science and technology, including Drama and Science.

http://www.psci-com.ac.uk/browse/detail/205b8c9a6b18d476abc94908e0280ea5.html

- Drama as a Teaching Tool in Bioethics:
  http://bio.ltsn.ac.uk/events/reports/stirling2003ethic.htm#drama
- The YMCA's *Y Touring* theatre group.
  http://www.ytouring.org.uk/science/
- The BBC has a range of resources such as their video nation archives which has sections on beliefs, health, and values:
  http://www.bbc.co.uk/videonation/archive/.

iii. Narrative

Discussion of morally sensitive issues can become over-heated if it is handled incorrectly. This is of particular concern when students are asked to draw on their own experience to provide cases or scenarios for consideration for they will then have a personal stake in the subject matter. In general, a moderate distance from the issues is conducive to a balanced and constructive debate. One advantage of using  narrative (drawn from books, films television *etc.*) over stories drawn from personal experience is that it allows a degree of emotional or empathic response without the close identification that one gets when people describe their own actions, or actions that have impacted on them personally.

There is some overlap between the use of drama and role-play discussed in the preceding section and the use of narrative, but narrative drawn from films, plays and television dramas/documentaries is fixed and therefore not susceptible to direct student interaction. However, it can be equally productive as a stimulus to debate and discussion, both verbal and written, of the issues raised. Further, narrative is not limited to dramatic forms but extends to include the use of other written texts (both fictional and biographical and poetic) plus visual art (both painting and photographic).

In many cases, the student may have prior experience of the narrative resource, and it can be instructive for them to contrast their previous reaction to the more reflective response prompted by a narrative-based ethics learning and teaching module. Narratives that are already in the public domain can be discussed without concern over the infringement of confidentiality or informed consent requirements. Since many texts are normally read for pleasure, pre-seminar reading is more likely to have been done, and done thoroughly.

Written texts such as novels or biographies, with their intense and detailed depiction of a person's inner life, can offer an excellent way of conveying the nebulous nature of real-life ethical decision-making; a realisation that learners in Higher Education have normally reached with respect to their private lives but which does not always get translated into the professional domain. In the past, professional ethics learning and teaching has sometime reinforced this division but over recent years there have been moves to a more holistic interpretation. For example within medicine, instead of a conception of the patient as 'the appendectomy in bed three', one now begins to find an appreciation of the fact that:

> [I]n the context of a patient's life … sets of consequences and options are usually fuzzy and open. The role of narrative ethics as a supplement to virtue ethics (and the ethics of care popular in nursing circles) is to handle decision-making in the context of a patient's life-story; something which is rarely, if ever, linear.[86]

The link between the concept of a service-user's life *story* their tendency to perceive their own real experiences as a narrative and the use of written or dramatic texts is a key concept in the use of narrative as a learning and teaching method.

Modules designed with these objectives in mind aim to develop empathy by encouraging the use of 'thick' descriptions in which the students' own emotional reactions to the case and the client's character or family circumstances are all admitted as relevant factors in moral deliberation.[87]

Visual texts such as drama or iconic images can be an excellent resource for sensitising students to the importance of non-verbal communication when considering ethical issues. For example, radiographers are required to be,

> aware of the characteristics and consequences of non-verbal communication and how this can be affected by culture, age, ethnicity, gender, religious beliefs and socio-economic status.[88]

An appreciation of these issues can be developed either by viewing visual images (both static and moving) or by reading a text with reference to the way the author indicates a character's feelings or characteristics through descriptions of their behaviour or body language.

Students need not be restricted to the discussion of existing sources, but can be encouraged to explore issues creatively, by producing their own narratives in the form of short stories or poems, or by selecting images that have particular relevance to themselves.

All links are available live at http://www.prs-ltsn.ac.uk/ethics

[86] Ashcroft, R.E. (2000) *op. cit.*

[87] Carson A.M. (2001) "That's another story: narrative methods and ethical practice", *Journal of Medical Ethics*, vol. 27, no. 3, pp. 198-202(5)

[88] http://www.hpc-uk.org/publications/standards_of_proficiency_ra.htm

Narrative texts and resources can be used in many ways, but in general terms there are a number of learning outcomes that they can be expected to serve:

- Allow students to consider ethical issues as one aspect or dimension of a complex situation in which action depends not only on the outcome of a moral decision but on other significant factors.
- Encourage the use of 'thick' descriptions that draw on personal characteristics, social relations and emotional states in addition to ethical concepts and principles.
- Encourage an appreciation of multiple-perspectives on contested issues.
- Develop empathy.
- Promote a balance between personal engagement with the issues and objective evaluation.
- Allow the use of imagination in concert with reason in the formulation of ethically significant courses of action.
- Facilitate the application of a variety of learning styles to ethics learning and teaching.
- Promote a service-user-centred approach.
- Promote a holistic view of persons (professional, service-user and others).

The Ethicist's Tale: Using the Humanities to Facilitate Learning in Healthcare

Deborah Bowman
St George's Hospital Medical School

Perhaps one of the greatest challenges for all teachers and learners is to remain imaginative about education: for teachers to avoid the safety of using only well-tried teaching methods and for students to avoid the temptation to become passive recipients of information. Although this is an educational challenge for all those involved in teaching and learning, the challenge can be particularly acute for those training healthcare professionals where there is frequently an already crammed curriculum and a great deal of 'information' to be both delivered and learned (though, of course, the two things do not always seamlessly merge). This paper considers the use of humanities as one imaginative device for facilitating learning in healthcare ethics and argues that narrative and emotion are powerful tools for engaging teachers and learners alike.

Humanities in Healthcare Education

The place of humanities in healthcare education has a relatively recent history. Even in the United States (which is frequently seen as the place in which the 'medical humanities' movement began), the subject only really began to take its place in faculties and on curricula in the 1970s. In the United Kingdom, there has been increasing interest in the use of humanities in healthcare education in the last decade. Much of this work has been led by Dr Deborah Kirklin and her colleagues at the UCH and the Royal Free Medical School and Dr Jane McNaughton who is the Director of the Centre for Arts and Humanities in Health and Medicine at the University of Durham.

Ethics and Humanities

Is there a natural link between healthcare ethics and humanities? Perhaps it is worth considering first of all the ways in which the subject of 'healthcare ethics' is constructed and understood. Is the subject of 'healthcare ethics':

- A branch of moral philosophy?
- A close relation of medical law?
- An historical and social perspective on professional rules and regulations?
- A sub-set of a broader subject that might be called 'medical humanities' or the human and behavioural aspects of healthcare
- None or all of the above?

It may be that whatever one believes one is teaching when delivering seminars, courses and lectures in 'healthcare ethics', the importance of emotion and the power of the narrative is greatly under-developed in, but a nonetheless essential aspect of, the business of moral reasoning.

Indeed if one accepts, that the aims of healthcare education are to produce practitioners who are reflective, empathetic and humane, professional, patient-centred, honourable and responsible, drawing on emotion and offering contrasting human perspectives on moral dilemmas in healthcare may be an essential part of ethics teaching and learning. Medical humanities offers an innovative approach by which to engage students AND staff in reflection on values and development of virtue in education. In particular, humanities can:-

- Accentuate the power of the narrative in healthcare ethics (thereby reminding all that healthcare is a human science and engaging learners)
- Offer multiple perspectives on a dilemma or problem
- Capture the 'silent' or overlooked perspectives in ethics
- Make emotion and psychological responses an explicit and integral part of what constitutes a practitioner's 'duty of care'

Using humanities in healthcare teaching and learning 'on the ground'

At St George's Hospital Medical School, we have experimented with the use of humanities in teaching and learning. Some of the activities tried include:

- Students selecting and bringing their own fictional and non-fictional accounts of mental illness to ethics seminars in mental health
- Special Study Modules in music and medicine, art and healthcare and literature and medicine
- Core clinical teaching in psychiatry includes representations of mental illness and psychiatrists in film
- Including fictional and autobiographical reading on the standard reference list for most Problem Based Learning tutorials e.g. Gearin Tosh for a tutorial concerning multiple myeloma, Ruth Picardie and John Diamond for tutorials concerning cancer and Lauren Slater for a tutorial concerning epilepsy. Students are encouraged to make their own recommendations for inclusion on reference lists.
- Excerpts from Jed Mercurio's 'Bodies' provide trigger materials for seminars on 'duties of care', 'whistleblowing' and 'self-care'
- Atul Gawande's 'Complications' provides trigger material for a seminar on uncertainty
- Staff/student trip to see 'Blue Orange' as part of psychiatric ethics module
- Staff/student trip to see 'The Talking Cure' at National Theatre
- Anatomy/ethics trip to 'Bodyworlds' exhibition followed up by discussion of dignity in death and consent for post-mortems

To date, using humanities has proved advantageous in three principal ways. First, students appear to value innovation and variety in teaching. Enhanced engagement and enthusiasm is perhaps the greatest incentive of all to continue developing the place of humanities in applied ethics teaching. The benefits are not simply limited to enhanced student engagement however. Secondly, teachers and academics enjoy considerable personal and professional development by expanding their knowledge and skills base and perhaps revisiting familiar ideas from a new perspective or in an original context. Refreshed teachers are generally better and happier teachers! Finally, the use of humanities revives the importance of the narrative in healthcare ethics and reminds us all, that just as medicine is a human science, so healthcare ethics is concerned with the application of philosophy to human dilemmas and experiences. In the words of Hudson-Jones (1999) narrative in ethics requires readers to consider whether the patient is ultimately the author of his own text.

Humanities and Healthcare Resources

Perhaps the most important resources for anyone interested in using humanities in teaching applied ethics are other people: staff and students who read, attend the theatre, listen to and play music, visit art exhibitions, paint and draw are all potent sources of inspiration. Beyond the many resources that surround each of us in the form of colleagues and students, there are some other useful resources. The Journal of Medical Ethics has a discrete medical humanities supplement called the Journal of Medical Humanities. Other teaching and learning journals such as 'Medical Education' have features on the use of humanities. On the internet, the huge and impressive resource[89] from New York University is unsurpassed although largely limited to literature. Finally, there is a UK project based on the New York University resource.[90]

Humanities and Healthcare Ethics: The Future

Presently, humanities in the education of healthcare professionals is at a relatively nascent stage of development. The challenges that face those enthusiastic about the inclusion of the humanities in teaching and learning include developing scholarship, evaluating outcomes and training staff and students to feel confident about facilitating some of the emotional responses that can occur when powerful and touching materials are used in teaching and learning

If there is a mass of interested academics in UK who are keen to develop their skills and interest in this area, perhaps it is time that we begin work on a nation wide exchange of ideas, experiences and resources. Such a network should extend beyond the exchanging of cards in a flurry of enthusiasm at a conference. So to those with whom I exchanged cards at the LTSN workshop, please send me an e-mail!

All links are available live at http://www.prs-ltsn.ac.uk/ethics

[89] http://endeavour.med.nyu.edu/lit-med/
[90] http://www.mhrd.ucl.ac.uk/

A Case Study

Students would be asked to read the following story.

In the Name of the Mother, the Son and the Holy Ghost

It was only twenty two days since the baby's premature birth but already the sights, sounds and smells of the Special Care Baby Unit had become as the familiar to Janice as those of her own kitchen. For the first week, when her daughter Lisa had been too ill to leave her bed, Janice had had the clear plastic box and its fragile contents to herself, so that by now baby Reading seemed more like her son than her grandson. She had even named him in the privacy of her own head—calling him Paul after her much missed elder brother.

The second week had seen the first of Lisa's visits and had been a precious time of mutual support but with Week Three had come a sudden twist of discord. The medical staff had begun, through carefully phrased hints and indications, to prepare them for the likelihood that baby Reading would not see the end of his first month and after an initial half-hour of shared anguish the whispered arguments between mother and daughter had started. Janice wanted to baptise her grandson but Lisa was adamant that this would not be done.

Janice found Lisa's attitude difficult to understand; her own Catholic faith was a source of comfort at times like this, offering an assurance of the ultimate purpose of seemingly random events, and the promise of reunion in the face of imminent loss. Lisa's religious observance had been patchy since her teens but Janice blamed this on her son-in-law—a nice enough lad but as far as religion was concerned he said he was C. of E. and everyone knew what *that* meant. Lisa had still been keen enough to have a nuptial mass for her wedding day and in the complication-free first trimester of her pregnancy, had raised no objections to Janice's talk of the big 'Do' for the christening of the first grandchild. They had even picked out a gown for the baby—all lace and elaborate stitching—but Lisa had refused to allow Janice to buy it before the birth, saying that she didn't want to tempt fate.

Now everything had changed. Sometimes Lisa said that God wouldn't be so cruel as to condemn an innocent baby to Limbo. At other times, she said that if there *was* a God, why would he be so wicked as to let her baby die? At all times she was clear that there would be no anointing, no water, no 'renouncing of the Devil'. It would be like accepting that the baby had no chance at all and he *did* have a chance. He was getting stronger every day. The doctors didn't say that he couldn't live—only that it was touch and go. Lisa would never give up hope, no matter what her mother might say.

These were thoughts that thronged inside Janice's head as she sat beside the incubator and watched the tiny lungs battle against failing strength. Lisa was asleep on the sideward so Janice had Paul to herself for a while. She wasn't sure for how long—maybe thirty minutes, maybe an hour if she was lucky then Lisa would be back to join the vigil and maintain a guard. Suddenly was it clear to Janice what she must do. The resolution presented itself, whole and fully formed, from the apparent chaos of her subconscious mind.

She picked up the plastic cup of water that one of the nurses had brought her earlier. Its contents were at room temperature, which meant 28°C in the overheated atmosphere of the baby unit. The only snag was that she needed to raise the lid of the incubator and was afraid of setting off the alarm.

At the other side of the room was a nurse—a tall well-spoken girl in her late twenties, and the one with whom Lisa had established the greatest rapport.

'Nurse!' Janice called softly, 'Nurse Emma.'

Emma sighed to herself and mentally postponed her cup of tea yet again.

'Yes Mrs Phillips?' she responded, padding across in sensible shoes. 'How are you doing?'

'Coping.' Janice smiled and Emma saw exhaustion etched into every feature. 'For now at least.' Janice hesitated, her hands squeezing the plastic cup so tightly that its contents rose up and threatened to overspill. 'I wanted to ask your favour.'

'Of course,' the nurse replied cautiously, 'if I can.'

'I want you to raise the lid on the incubator.'

Emma said nothing but her face was eloquent with doubt and concern.

'I want to baptised him,' Janice nodded towards the sleeping child. 'Before it's too late.'

For a moment Emma maintained her silence, then she took a deep breath and began slowly,

'But Mrs Phillips ...'

'There's no danger,' Janice interrupted, one eye on the door where her daughter might appear at any moment. 'All I need to do is pour a little water over his forehead—just a drop, only the tiniest drop—and say a few words.'

'But Mrs Phillips—Janice ...' Emma reached out to put a placatory hand on Janice's arm.

'It won't take long,' said Janice. 'No more than fifteen seconds.' Her voice was rising now, sensing opposition. 'The incubator is open for much longer than that when you're washing him.'

'I know, but—.'

'I don't need a priest or anything. My religion allows anyone to do it *in extremis.*'

'I know—.'

'Then you must understand what it means to me—to him—to be baptised before he dies,' Janice urged. 'All I have to do you is say "I baptise thee Paul"—that's the name I've given him, Paul after my brother— "I baptise thee Paul in the name of the Father, Son, and Holy Ghost." Then a little water poured over his head and it's done. What harm can it do?'

'That's not the point,' Emma said firmly. Her grip on Janice's arm changed from comfort to one of gentle control. 'Why don't you come through to the Relatives' Room? We can talk better there. Or I could call a priest to counsel you.'

'It isn't me that needs the priest' Janice wailed, tears of frustration welling into her eyes. 'And there isn't time to talk about it. Lisa could be here at any minute.'

'Yes and that *is* the point.' Emma stood back and folded her arms across her chest, her gaze shifting to her patient. 'I'm sorry Janice—I do understand that this is very difficult for you but you know very well that Mrs Reading doesn't want her baby baptised just yet, and she *is* his mother. It's her decision, not yours.'

'She doesn't mean it.' Janice took a deep breath to suppress the sobs that were constricting her throat and making it difficult to speak. 'She's angry and in pain right now, but when all this is over and the baby is dead she'll wish she'd done the right thing.'

'What about now?' Emma asked quietly. 'Shouldn't you consider what Lisa needs right now?'

'She needs her baby to live but you can't give her that and neither can I.'

'There's always hope, Mrs Phillips. And if the worst happens—well the human mind has great powers of recuperation, but your daughter will need all your support. If you make her feel guilty—.'

'Do you really think I would?' Janice cried. 'I'd never say a word—not when it was too late—but I wouldn't need to. Once a Catholic, always a Catholic. Her beliefs are still there, whatever she might say and in the long run it will kill her to know that she kept her son out of heaven.'

'Mrs Phillips! Please!' Emma was bitterly regretting having started this conversation and knew that she was way out of her depth. An agnostic herself, she was generally tolerant of religious belief in others, but she found Janice's acceptance of a God who would condemn a baby on such trivial grounds repugnant. 'I really think that we should go through to the Relatives Room. I'll make some tea and ask the priest come round as soon as possible. I'm sure there must be some other way to set your mind rest—.'

'There's no other way,' said Janice miserably. She thought for a moment then tried a different tack. 'What about the father?' she suggested. 'My son-in-law said he didn't mind the child going to a Catholic school—.'

'All this is for Mr and Mrs Reading to decide,' Emma insisted, taking Janice by the shoulder and steering her firmly towards the door. 'Now come and sit yourself down. Perhaps your daughter will agree to speak to the priest with you—it might help her if you are correct about her true feelings. But I hope you understand that we can't override Lisa's wishes in this. It wouldn't be right.'

Janice paused and made her final appeal.

'She needn't know,' she whispered. 'Let me baptise the baby now, without telling her. And I'll never tell her—not unless she regrets refusing to do it herself. Just think about Lisa and how she'll feel when she does change her mind and it's too late. Think how it will prey on her conscience. Help me now so I can help her then—I'll be able to tell her not to worry—that the baby *was* baptised—that he is happy in heaven. And if she never changes her mind I won't say a word—not to my dying day.'

Emma hesitated. It made a sense of a kind and she found it difficult to account for her own reluctance, but the bottom line was that the parents said "No" and that was all there was to it.

'You could always lie,' she said at last.

'What?'

'If your daughter regrets not baptising the baby, you could tell her that you had done it.'

'But it wouldn't be true.'

'Would that matter if it gave Lisa peace of mind?'

Janice shook her head and admitted defeat.

'You just don't understand—you're not a Catholic.'

'No, Mrs Phillips I'm a nurse. I'm really sorry but I have to put the baby and his parents first.'

And with that she led Janice over to an armchair then went to put the kettle on.

Ethical Issues

- The Duty of Care:
  - To whom is it owed?
  - What obligations does the nurse have in situations where there is no clinical decision to be made?
- Respect for religious sensitivities.
- Multiple conceptions of the patient's best interests.
- Conflicts of interests.

Using the Case Study with Students

There are a number of issues that have a moral dimension in the above story, but a key difference between the embedded approach and the pragmatic and theoretical ones is that there need be no overt reference to ethics or morality in either the story itself or the students' consideration of the story.

It may also be noted that although the nurse is asked to make a morally sensitive decision, it does not relate to an aspect of *medical* ethics as there is no clinical decision to be made about the best interests of the patient. It does, however, highlight the difficulty of interpreting the Duty of Care as defined in the notion of Fitness for Practice.

For example, to whom is the duty of care owed?

To the baby and his mother the duty is owed in respect of their position as patients within the hospital. Lisa might claim an additional claim as the parent of a minor but what about Janice? Does she have a claim at all, and if so, is it a direct claim that the staff should consider her welfare or does she have only an indirect claim based on her contribution to the welfare of the baby and his mother? Can one formulate a general position with respect to grandparents of premature babies or can one only answer the question by reference to the individual circumstances of this case such as Janice's three-week presence on the ward, her character, and her relationship with her daughter.

These are complicated and deeply interrelated questions, and exploration via narrative formats will sometimes be the best way for students to tackle them.

Facilitators can invite students to consider whether the nurse's behaviour is defensible by reference to overtly ethical concepts and principles, but this is not essential. More important is that they explore their own reactions to the story. There are a number of prompts or questions that might be posed to help them do this:

- With whom do they identify most in this story?
- Do their sympathies change as the narrative unfolds?
- What kind of people are Janice, Emma and Lisa?
- If Lisa's unnamed husband had been involved would he have had a different perspective on the situation?
- Would they have acted as Emma did?
- If not, in what way were their actions have differed?
- What difference might it have made if the nurse had shared Janice's religious beliefs?

If the narrative is presented within a group discussion format it is also worth students asking themselves: *Does their reading of the story change as a result of group discussion?*

An enquiry along these lines will bring out much that is ethically relevant in the students' attitudes, and the teacher may choose to bring these aspects to their attention for overt consideration. Indications that students are not applying their ethical values or principles consistently or that they have difficulty in stating the moral issues embedded within the story would identify areas where there is potential for the student to learn and enrich their capacity to behave ethically.

Alternatively, if the embedded format is used to serve embedded learning objectives, the narrative would be used to explore and enrich the students conception of what it means to be 'Fit to

Practice'. The ethical dimension would be examined in concert with other factors through their consideration of a story in which ethical principles and concepts are embedded, but would not be treated to separate and overt consideration. Indications that a student's conception of Fitness to Practice is incompatible with the requirements of registration as assessed at their institution, will identify areas where there is potential for the student to learn and develop their views.

Theoretical Approaches to Ethics

I want to know what it is like for a *bat* to be a bat …
Thomas Nagel, *Mortal Questions*

What is it like to be a rat?

The trouble is not … that human concepts cannot be extended to other species. It is that such extensions must be done sensitively. Apparently similar patterns can play very different parts in the lives of different species.
Mary Midgley, *Beast & Man*

I do not wish [women] to have power over men; but over themselves.
Mary Wollstonecraft, *A Vindication of the Rights of Woman*

Whose Right is it anyway?

Every community has a right to demand of all its agents, an account of their conduct.
Tom Paine, *The Rights of Man*

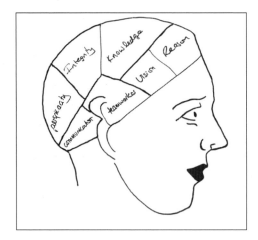

So the good has been well explained as being that at which all things aim.
Aristotle, *Nicomachean Ethics*

The Virtues of the Professional

For Aristotle, each of the virtues is an organized way of cherishing a particular end that has intrinsic value.
Martha Nussbaum, *Virtue Ethics: a misleading category?*

Theoretical

Introduction

Ethics in its broadest sense is perhaps more properly regarded as supradisciplinary than interdisciplinary, for it is concerned with human actions and agency and as such, has relevance to all areas of human endeavour. Within learning and teaching, there is an assumption that learning itself is a moral endeavour but ethics is often marginal as an overt discipline. Implied values are not made clear and are often unsupported by coherent and consistent arguments. Learning and teaching which takes as its primary objective the overt statement of these implied values facilitates scrutiny and provides a sound basis for debate regarding the role of moral values in education as a whole, and in the evolution of ethics education across the curriculum.

Taking a theoretical approach to ethics learning and teaching means starting with a study of ethical theory; the concepts, principles, and arguments that underpin the Codes of Practice considered in the pragmatic approach and the notions of the Professional behaviour and Fitness to Practice considered in the embedded approach.

It can be argued that a deep understanding of ethics as applied to any discipline requires some attention to theory, but the experience of teachers working outside disciplines such as philosophy and religious studies suggests that the theoretical approach is the one which students are least likely to relate to the rest of their studies and their future working lives. Where ethics is taught on an elective basis this might not be a problem provided there are enough students with an aptitude for conceptual analysis and the consideration of normative issues to make the module viable. However professional ethics will often be mandatory, either as a separate module or as a component in a broader syllabus, so the difficulties many students find in the theoretical approach must be taken seriously.

It is not possible within a guide of this type to offer a comprehensive review of theoretical approaches to learning and teaching in ethics. The theoretical approach has a tradition dating back over two thousand years and is a core component of the curriculum for any department of philosophy or theology. In addition, most taught post-graduate courses in professional ethics will make significant use of moral theory. This section will therefore be confined to three areas that may be of interest to teachers of ethics across the curriculum.

Firstly, it will consider the role of theory in issues-based ethics teaching. Secondly, it will outline the key differences between the theoretical approach and the pragmatic/embedded approaches in respect of learning and teaching objectives. Thirdly it will consider the key skills that may be enhanced by adopting a theoretical approach.

While students from disciplines outside philosophy and religious studies may study ethics without making any use of the theoretical approach, it is arguable that those with a responsibility for teaching ethics in whatever format need some acquaintance with the more abstract conceptual forms of analysis on which it depends since it is principally through this medium that discussion about how ethics can and should be taught across the curriculum is carried out. A guest contribution from Rev. Dr John Strain, Director of Federal University of Surrey Centre for Applied and Professional Ethics provides an example of this type of discourse when he asks '*What is distinctive about ethics in particular disciplinary practices and what is transferable across disciplines?*'.

The final part of this section provides an example of a case study as it might be used within the theoretical approach.

Issue-Based Learning

The more influential science becomes, the more ethical issues become associated with scientific practice directly, and scientists are increasingly required to participate in the value questions born from new knowledge and new technologies.[91]

The pragmatic approach has been considered in the context of disciplines with a strong research component, while Fitness for Practice and Professionalism is of particular importance to graduates from subject areas feeding the service professions. However many subjects will have some area of enquiry or application that arouses public concern and many benchmarking statements reflect this by requiring that graduates have some understanding of ethical issues of significance to their subject area and the ability to contribute to debate on these issues. For example, the benchmark statement for Bioscience states that:

Whatever the subject discipline, students should expect to be confronted by some of the scientific, moral and ethical questions raised by their study discipline, to consider viewpoints other than their own, and to engage in critical assessment and intellectual argument.[92]

All links are available live at http://www.prs-ltsn.ac.uk/ethics

[91] Clarkeburn H.; Downie J.R.; Matthew B. (2002) 'Impact of an Ethics Programme in a Life Sciences Curriculum', *Teaching in Higher Education*, Vol. 7, no. 1, pp. 65-79
[92] http://www.qaa.ac.uk/crntwork/benchmark/phase2/biosciences.pdf

For Veterinary Medicine:

graduates must … be able to construct reasoned arguments to support their actions and positions on the ethical and social impact of veterinary science and the allied biosciences. [93]

For Occupational Therapy:

The graduate occupational therapist must … treat individuals with respect and draw on ethical principles in the process of reasoning.[94]

For Pharmacists, the graduate

must be able to recognise ethical dilemmas in healthcare and science and understand ways in which these might be managed by healthcare professionals, whilst taking account of relevant law.[95]

In order to fulfil this requirement, students must be able to give overt consideration to moral questions. This means being able to:

- Recognise ethically sensitive issues.
- Identify and describe their ethical dimension.
- Distinguish ethical issues from associated non-moral factors such as matters of fact or of law.
- Formulate the relevant moral arguments, both for and against.
- Offer a balanced appraisal of the relative merits of these arguments
- Present their views in terms appropriate to public debate.

This approach contrasts strongly with the embedded one, in that it seeks to abstract and isolate moral issues, as far as possible; to provide a 'thin' description that eschews personal context, emotional content and the specifics of an individual situation.

The main difference between a consideration of these issues within departments of philosophy or religious studies and that found in other faculties such as science relates to the primary domain of expertise. For example, in a controversial area of enquiry such as xenotransplantation, a bioscience student can be expected to have a

---

All links are available live at http://www.prs-ltsn.ac.uk/ethics

[93] http://www.qaa.ac.uk/crntwork/benchmark/phase2/vet_sci.pdf, p.7

[94] http://www.qaa.ac.uk/crntwork/benchmark/nhsbenchmark/ot.pdf, p.15

[95] http://www.rpsgb.org.uk/pdfs/compfutphwfph1s6.pdf

good grasp of the science, but will lack the depth of moral theory that might be expected of a philosophy student, while for the philosophy student the converse is true.

Issues-based learning and teaching in ethics will therefore require careful identification of the students' expected strengths and weaknesses in approaching the topic, to determine which aspects of the issue can be apportioned to the students for their own research, and which areas will require more input and guidance from the teachers.

Ethics and Philosophy

The theoretical tradition of applied/professional ethics teaching has the longest history within Higher Education as it is the approach taken within departments of philosophy, theology and religious studies for whom ethics has been a core subject from the outset. Departments of Law also take a theoretical approach designed to give students an understanding of the moral arguments and principles that were instrumental in the formulation of legislation, and which have an ongoing role in its interpretation.

Students within these departments approach applied ethics by first considering the relevant concepts, principles and arguments of moral theory to provide a framework within which particular cases can be located and analysed. This strong theoretical foundation is itself grounded in core modules that provide a broader conceptual and methodological framework from a consideration of subjects such as logic and theory of knowledge, and the acquisition of broadly based analytical and reasoning skills.

Only when students have attained a sound grasp of moral theory will they be asked to apply it to real-life or life-like situations. The function of applied ethics within this context is not to prepare students to cope with those situations in real life, but rather a means of deepening of their understanding of moral theory through a consideration of its application to human action in specific situations.

Though much of the language used in this environment would not be familiar to those based in other departments, the key processes of conceptual analysis, reasoning and argument would not be regarded as a barrier to discourse with people from other disciplines, but as a way of breaking down such barriers. Learning and teaching objectives would, accordingly, focus on developing those abilities deemed essential to anyone wishing to address ethical issues in a rational, transparent and consistent way and would normally include one or more of the following:

- Development of critical reasoning faculties.

- Application of moral theories such as Rights, Virtue Ethics, Consequentialism or Kantian deontology to real-life situations[96].
- Identification and analysis of morally challenging situations.
- Acquisition of a facility with the language of moral discourse.
- Awareness of multiple perspectives on contested issues.
- Development of coherent principles of thought and action.
- Capacity for verbal and written presentation.

Modules based on this tradition do not seek to persuade students of the merits of a particular set of moral beliefs, or motivate them to attain predefined standards of behaviour. In this respect they form a marked contrast with modules in which the student's knowledge of ethics is a means to the end of shaping their actions as future professionals. Even where courses are not overtly prescriptive, there can be an implicit intention to go beyond the delivery of a body of knowledge; to enter the realm of character development and the promotion of professional virtues.

Rest defined a four component model for moral behaviour:

1) Moral sensitivity
2) Moral judgement
3) Moral motivation
4) Moral character. [97]

The enhancement of moral judgement is common to all three approaches although it may not be referred to explicitly in the pragmatic and embedded forms.
So too is moral sensitivity,

> a practical skill that enables one to recognize when an act, situation or certain aspects of a situation have moral implications. [98]

All links are available live at http://www.prs-ltsn.ac.uk/ethics

[96] **Rights:** Rights define the benefits that other people or society should provide for the right-holder. Rights can be negative, stating what others may *not* do, as well as positive, stating what they may do.

Virtue Ethics: A theory in which moral value is derived from the character of the moral agent.

Consequentialism: Any theory in which the moral worth of an action is measured in terms of its consequences .

Kantian Deontology: A theory is deontological if moral worth depends on the agent's motives for acting. Immanual Kant argued that a moral motive was one which was derived from the agent's sense of duty.

[97] Rest, J. R. (1983). Morality. In Mussen, P. H. (ser. ed.), Flavell, J., and Markman, E. (vol. eds.), *Handbook of Child Psychology: Cognitive Development*, Vol. 3, Wiley, New York, pp. 556-629

[98] Jaeger S.M. (2001) 'Teaching health care ethics: the importance of moral sensitivity for moral reasoning', *Nursing Philosophy*, vol. 2, no. 2, pp. 131-142

Where the approaches differ is in the attention paid to moral motivation and character. Moral motivation involves prioritising the moral over other significant concerns, while moral character means being able to construct and implement actions that service the morally desirable choice. Both these elements of moral behaviour are frequently addressed within pragmatic and embedded learning and teaching, and modules from this domain will normally serve one or more of the following outcomes:

- Apply research guidelines or a professional code.
- Promote good professional conduct.
- Engage in reflective practice.
- Explore background moral beliefs.
- Develop empathy.
- Help students perceive a particular choice or course of action as the correct one, where that correct course of action is determined by reference to such things as:
  - Government Legislation and Guidelines.
  - Professional code(s) of conduct.
  - Research Guidelines.
  - Canonical Text(s).

Insofar as these learning outcomes refer to morally desirable *behaviour* they would be considered inappropriate to a philosophical approach. McNulty states that:

> [p]hilosophers are ill-suited to the role of moral guidance. Instead they should set out to instil in students the necessity of being able to formulate rational bases for moral views.[99]

Similarly, within philosophical medical ethics Gillon rules out the quoting or drawing up of professional codes of conduct, accounts of the legal constraints on doctors' behaviour and the expression of religious rules or sentiments.[100] Instead, there is an emphasis on analysis and a critical examination of "*concepts, assumptions, beliefs, attitudes, emotions, reasons, and arguments*".[101]

It is therefore important for teachers combining material from more than one approach to be clear about their learning and teaching objectives in different parts of the course, not only as a means of ensuring that these objectives are met but as a way of anticipating

---

All links are available live at http://www.prs-ltsn.ac.uk/ethics

[99] McNulty M. (2002) Teaching Applied Ethics Effectively, *Teaching Philosophy*, Volume 21, Number 4, pp. 361-372

[100] Gillon R. (1999) *Philosophical Medical Ethics*, John Wiley & Sons: Chichester. p.1.

[101] *Ibid.* p.2.

potential conflict between them. For example, a pragmatic approach, in which students accept the mandates of a professional code of practice as 'given' might militate against learning and teaching format based on the 'theoretical' objectives of critical evaluation of assumptions and arguments. These potential conflicts between the approaches are symptomatic of tensions within ethics teaching across the curriculum as a whole.

Ethics and Key Skills

Learning and teaching via the theoretical approach enhances teaches a number of transferable skills.

- Analytical Skills: A consideration of Moral Theory develops an aptitude for clear and logical thought. Students learn to think critically and break down complex problems.
- Flexibility and Independence of Mind: Moral Theorists must be able to consider issues from multiple perspectives. A willingness to challenge orthodoxies is encouraged, as is the value of setting aside one's own personal convictions to pursue an argument wherever it might lead.
- Decision Making: Moral Theorists search for coherent principles of thought and action and learn to determine what kinds of evidence are needed to support their views and choices.
- Communication skills: Moral Theory students must learn to express their views verbally and in writing. There is an emphasis on group discussion and the articulation of arguments in direct response to verbal questions and critiques.

In so far as an applied/professional ethics module takes a broadly theoretical approach to its subject matter, it can be expected to enhance the students' facility with the key skills listed above. For students whose primary area of study lies outside philosophy, theology *etc.* at least some of these skills will not be developed to the same degree by the rest of their coursework.

The study of ethics also introduces the consideration of *values* and this is potentially of even greater importance to the graduate's performance in a work environment because a professional needs to do more than decide what their options are and how those options can be put into practice; they must also decide what *ought* to be done. A professional who has learned to recognise, define and justify value judgements will therefore be a more effective decision-maker than one who lacks these skills. Ethics training can be of particular benefit to students from science and technology where the emphasis on implementation and problem solving means that students would otherwise have very little opportunity to consider embedded concepts and values.

Care, knowledge and design in professional practice[102]

John Strain

Director, Federal University of Surrey Centre for Applied and Professional Ethics

> *Broadly my thesis is that three particular concepts: care, knowledge and design figure necessarily as common features in the ethics of all professional practices. But the precise way in which these concepts relate together provide for the variety and difference between different professional practices.*

Noddings (2003) proposes an ethic of caring in which relationships between people, not individual people themselves, have an ontological primacy. Noddings wrote as an educationalist rather than as a healthcare professional but the ethics of care has been taken up with some enthusiasm within nursing by, amongst others, Benner and Wrubel (1989), and Johnstone (1994). Tschudin (2003:1) suggests that *"caring is not unique to nursing, but it is unique within nursing."* Part of what I want to suggest in this paper is that the mode in which care for people is expressed is unique to each professional practice. All professions are concerned with offering some service intended to benefit a client. In less utilitarian terms, we might say that some activity is conducted which the client has good reason to value. For professions are neither about harming people nor acting indifferently towards the interests of clients. To that extent there is some relationship of care between professional and client, a relationship which might be guarded, or not, through various legal embodiments such as duties of care in common law or by contractual obligations of care.

But there is clearly more to being a professional than caring for another in a relationship. What distinguishes a professional relationship from a marriage relationship or a close friendship is that the relationship is bounded by a particular domain of practice and by a body of well founded knowledge associated with that practice. A nurse, doctor, architect or school teacher has something to profess in the relationship with a client and the appropriateness of how a professional acts is in part determined by the well founded-ness of this knowledge. I use the term 'well founded' here to resist any particular purchase into 'scientific' or

---

All links are available live at http://www.prs-ltsn.ac.uk/ethics

[102] This is a revised version of a short paper delivered at the LTSN conference to help stimulate discussion. It presents what might be called a weak thesis for discussion about what is common and what is distinctive about ethics in different professional practices.

'positivistic' notions of knowledge. But at the same time nurses, doctors and architects must "know what they are talking about" in a manner beyond that demanded of armchair theorists and people on the Clapham omnibus.

The relationship between a professional's knowledge and the expression of care is often far from straightforward. Frequently, a doctor or nurse will take actions when there is very little knowledge of, or evidence for, the efficacy of the action in the particular circumstance. So care is not expressed simply by the exercise of knowledge. But experience and recognition of the relative risks of acting or taking no action are all deemed to count in the exercise of professional judgement. And they are what frequently distinguish professional action from the actions of caring people in the community.

The approach to knowledge taken by professionals is not quite the same as the approach taken by scientists or scholars. Scientists or scholars may be content that knowledge adds to (or perhaps replaces) existing theory or adds to the ways in which it is possible for people to comprehend phenomena. But for the professional, there is a more fundamental question: how can this knowledge help this client in this circumstance? There is some artefact, some process that needs to be designed for a client that is somehow 'fit for purpose' in relation to the client. This suggests a third key concept in what defines the professional: her or his concern to design something, an event, an artefact or a process which benefits the client and addresses the circumstance in which the client finds her or himself.

As well as identifying care, knowledge and design as key components of professional practice, there can also be identified a number of relationships between caring, knowledge and design which are common to all professionals. If whatever it is that the professional designs for the client is to address the client's circumstances, then some process of communication is necessary. Communication has a bearing on care and on knowledge. If the client is to place adequate trust in the professional to expose sufficient of his or her own vulnerable self for this communication to take place, then a sufficient relationship of care is required. The outcome of this communication for the professional needs to provide some basis for selecting, choosing or deciding upon whatever is to be designed for the client, based on well-founded knowledge. Thus communication, two-way communication is a link between care and both knowledge and design.

Another relationship between caring and knowledge concerns the process or journey of learning that takes place within the client. A patient's relationship with a nurse is in part a relationship of learning in which the client comes to understand the characteristics of, constraints upon, and opportunities for their own journeys of health, facilitated by the nurse or perhaps a doctor. A client's relationship with a solicitor is in part a learning journey for the client about the characteristics of the client's circumstances in regards to law, the constraints upon these circumstances and opportunities for the future.

The professional is thus an agent of other people's learning. What links the professor with the professional is that knowledge is professed in a way that others learn from it, either in the formal sense of the classroom, in the case of teacher, or through the process of understanding how one's needs and aspirations might be met by an artefact or process, the wisdom of adopting the artefact or process being grounded in knowledge. Both the architect and computing engineer begin with some notion of someone else's needs or aspirations. The owners of these needs and aspirations, the clients or patients go through some process of learning about how their aspirations can be realised. I am at pains here to be clear about how different these relationships with knowledge can be. For a teacher of science, an important aspect of how knowledge figures in his professional life is a respect due to the sheer facticity of things, things which are the case regardless of our feelings about, or our perception of them. But for a teacher of poetry an epistemology which stresses and helps articulate a child's response to a poem rather than a set of facts about the poem, may be particularly important.

These three concepts: caring for people, designing something for people and enlightening people through an interaction with knowledge are not altogether independent. The design of a building, process or product in seeking to realise the client's aspirations will often need to respect the laws of physics, mathematics or chemistry. An intrinsic component of caring for people will need to be sensitive to the learning journeys that patients or clients make when they articulate their needs.

Variations within the themes

The three themes of care, design and knowledge provide a canvas upon which many variations are possible for different professions. For some professions, particularly in healthcare, to care for persons means to hold them in an "unconditional positive regard", to use Carl Rogers words (1961). It reflects a commitment to the primacy of the perspective of those being cared for in a relationship in which the well-being of the person cared for is paramount. This is not an understanding of 'caring' which would come naturally to a consulting engineer or a computing engineer. But the codes of conduct of both these professions are quite incompatible with any idea that the client is not cared for or cared about. Amongst the seventeen rules in the Code of Conduct for Members of the British Computer Society, the first rule specifies the due care and diligence in accordance with the relevant authority's requirements, and the interests of system users that are to be safeguarded in the design of a computing system. Now, within the healthcare profession, and nursing in particular, caring for people has emerged as a defining component of professional identity. But as Hewitt (2002:434) remarks, drawing too close a link between ethics and caring risks conveying the suggestion that nurses are the only ethically oriented group in contact with patients. Doctors, healthcare professionals outside nursing as much as engineers and teachers all articulate some concept of care for people in their expressions of professional identity.

A clearer understanding of how care, design and knowledge for the professional might be gained by considering some examples of the different ways in which professionals care for clients. A nurse might see caring for a patient as demanding an almost exclusive focus and empathy on a patient's expression of pain. But caring for a patient entails a commitment to finding a remedy, a therapy, a way forward, all of which entail design and all of which must be well founded in knowledge. Where as all three, care, design and knowledge are important there is something natural about regarding a nurse as someone who focuses primarily on care, secondarily on design, and lastly on knowledge. But even here there may be differences across different categories of nursing and across contexts. Someone working with those approaching the end of their lives in a palliative care context might have little difficulty with the order of priorities of care, design and knowledge, whereas a nursing sister working in an operating theatre might in practice be far more concerned with following the procedures of a particular therapeutic design. But in both cases, the nurses might be seen as practitioners rather than the gatherers and guardians of well founded knowledge of bodily function and possibility. And medical doctors might be seen as focusing on knowledge, its medical validity and its applicability for the design of processes, but not to the extent that they could be accused of 'not caring for patients'.

It would hardly be considered ethical for a science teacher not to care about the pupils. But it might not be deemed unprofessional if limits were set to this care, limits set in terms of the safety and security of the child in the learning context and the teacher were then to invest energy in capturing the child's attention and cognition with the sheer wonder of knowledge, of physics or of chemistry. To do this, the teacher's primary activity might be the design of pedagogic steps in the curriculum, steps and devices that engender that sense of 'wow' in the child's mind that the world could be as fascinating as this. The teacher's care for the child is put into practice through designing and implementing a curriculum rather than through caring in the sense that a hospice nurse or psychotherapist might understand caring for a person. And the teacher, like the nurse, may be less directly concerned with knowledge.

An architect provides another example of how care, design and knowledge form components of professional practice. A commission begins with a client's brief, followed by a design to meet the requirements of the brief. But the architect is rarely chosen simply on his capability to meet the brief, but to bring a 'wow' factor to the design, a wow that stuns the client because the client had no idea a design that met the brief could look or feel quite like that. So the architect does not fail to care for his client's brief but is eager to put energy into aesthetics and design. The architect might also want to draw the client gently along the design journey so that the wow at the end is not a painful

These examples are intended to illustrate the different ways in which three key concepts of professional ethics, care, design and knowledge figure together in different ways in different professional practices.

Well, what's the significance of the claim that professional ethics differ across different professions according to the way that care, knowledge and design figure in different ways together? What's the impact on teaching and learning in ethics ? One important way of thinking about professional ethics is rooted in the Aristotelian tradition of virtue rather than the more recent, post Kantian tradition of principles. Virtue theory focuses on the acquisition and development of dispositions in the practitioner, dispositions that enable the practitioner to act with an appropriate emotional response, and which reflect the practitioner's acting with practical wisdom or phronesis in any circumstance. Virtuous action is action which can be characterized as lying between two vicious extremes. So acting with appropriate generosity, for example, lies between the vicious extremes of both profligacy and meanness. But how are these vicious extremes defined. They may, and indeed Aristotle suggests they will, vary in different practices. One possibility is that the meanings of care, knowledge and design help articulate these vicious extremes. A 'bookish' nurse may an unacceptable extreme for a nurse, in a way in which it would not be a vicious extreme for a engineering novice or schoolteacher. In short, we may need to go beyond care in understanding the demands of virtue in different professions.

References

Noddings, N (1984) Caring, a Feminine Approach to Ethics and Moral Education, 2003

Hewitt, J (2002) 'A critical review of the arguments debating the role of the nurse advocate' *Journal of Advanced Nursing*, 37 (5) 439-445

Tschudin (2003) *Ethics in Nursing, the Caring Relationship*, London, Butterworth, 1986, third edition 2003

Benner P & Wrubel J. (1989) *The Primacy of Caring* Addison Wesley, Menlo Park

Johnstone, M-J (1994) *Bioethics; a Nursing Perspective*, 2nd edition, Saunders, Marrickville, NSW

A Case Study

Scenario

Consider the following two cases:

Case One:

Ms X is 26 weeks pregnant. She has developed a medical condition, Z. If left untreated, Z poses a 75% risk of serious permanent damage to Ms X's health.

Ms X can be cured by a single oral administration of medication Med.1, but only if it is administered immediately, before the condition has a chance to progress. A side-effect of this treatment will be the death of the foetus and a miscarriage.

The foetus is currently healthy and is unlikely to be affected by condition Z, so if Ms X decides to reject treatment the prognosis for her pregnancy is that it will result in a healthy, full-term baby.

Case Two:

Ms A is 26 weeks pregnant. She has developed a medical condition, B, which means that if she continues with the pregnancy there is a 75% risk of serious permanent damage to Ms A's health.

The safest method of securing a termination for Ms A is a single oral administration of Med.2, which will cause the death of the foetus and induce a miscarriage.

The foetus is currently healthy and is unlikely to be affected by condition B, so if Ms A decides to reject treatment the prognosis for her pregnancy is that it will result in a healthy, full-term baby.

Ethical Issues

This scenario is designed to illustrate the Rule of Double Effect (RDE).

The RDE applies in cases where an action has two outcomes, one good and one bad. It would be located within the context of a consideration of whether actions should be evaluated purely on their consequences, or whether the agent's intensions have a moral significance which should be taken into account.

Where an agent performs an action that has good and bad consequences, does it matter whether the agent directly intends the bad consequence, or whether they merely foresee it? Some moral positions argue that it does, and apply the RDE to determine whether action is permissible.

The scenario above compares cases in which the actions and their consequences are similar; in each case treatment is administered that will cure a serious medical condition in a female patient, but which will also result in the death of a 26 week foetus that would otherwise be expected to develop into a healthy full-term baby. The cases differ with regard to the intentionality of the agent in respect of the bad effect.

Beauchamp and Childress[103] identify four necessary (and, taken together, sufficient) conditions for an act with a double effect to be permissible according to the RDE:

1) The act must be good, or at least morally neutral (independent of its consequences).
2) The agent must intend only the good effect.
3) The bad effect must not be a means to the good effect.
4) The good effect must outweigh the bad effect.

The scenario is designed to isolate point 3 by presenting cases that are similar in all but that respect.

In Case One there is no intension to cause the death of the foetus although it is a foreseeable consequence of treatment. If Ms X were not pregnant, or if the treatment had no effect on the foetus, there would still be a clinical reason to administer Med. 1 assuming that all the other conditions remained the same.

In Case Two, the agent intends only the good effect of curing Ms A (for they would not terminate the pregnancy if Ms A did not have the harmful medical condition) but this is achieved as a direct consequence of the bad effect. The bad effect is a means to the good effect. If Ms A were not pregnant, or if treatment had no effect on the foetus, there would be no clinical reason to administer Med. 2 assuming that all the other conditions remained the same.

Case One would therefore meet the conditions for permissible action subject to the RDE. Case Two would fail condition 3.

Using the Case Study with Students

In this Case Study, the scenario is used to illustrate a single condition in a specified principle. Students would be asked to accept, for the purposes of the illustration, that the good effect of curing a medical condition which carries a high risk of serious, permanent damage to the patient's health outweighs the bad effect of causing the death of a 26 week foetus.

In practice, this view would be challenged by those who regard the foetus as having the same value and rights as the mother (which would mean that both cases failed condition 4). Conversely, it might be argued that the death of the foetus was not a sufficiently bad

---

All links are available live at http://www.prs-ltsn.ac.uk/ethics

[103] Beauchamp, T.L. & Childress, J.F. (1994) *Principles of Biomedical Ethics*, Oxford:Oxford University Press, pp. 207

consequence to be considered significant in evaluating the moral consequences of treatment. Others might reject the RDE and require that the cases should be evaluated purely in terms of their consequences.

However, students are not being asked to reach a final conclusion on the moral justifiability of treatment, nor to decide what they themselves would do, but to explore how the application of the RDE might influence the outcome of the decision-making process. Using Case Studies via the theoretical approach will sometimes mean asking students to accept, for the purposes of argument or illustration, a moral position that they do not in fact hold, in order to understand the reasoning processes of people who have differing views from their own. In this case, they are asked to understand why those who regard intentions as being morally significant might make a distinction between Cases One and Two, allowing treatment to be morally justified in the first case but not the second.

Creating a Supportive Learning Environment

Students' Initial Expectations

Ethics is an essentially contested subject, and is capable of arousing powerful responses. Some students will have little or no experience of thinking about moral issues, or of debating them with others. This can give rise to a number of potential problems that should be anticipated by those responsible for devising course material aimed at students who are tackling ethics within Higher Education for the first time.

- Students might need help in order to realise that they already have opinions on moral issues.
- Students will sometimes find that the differences between an effective ethics learning framework and their accustomed discourse environment require some adjustment. If, for example, a seminar group is more culturally and socially diverse, or reflects a wider range of religious perspectives than they are used to, it may be necessary to establish rules or guidelines on appropriate and inappropriate modes of argument and self-expression.
- Modules may serve a wide student body with members representing several faculties, resulting in groups who are comparative strangers to one another with no pre-established grounds of mutual trust or confidence. Alternatively students could be drawn from a single course and know one another quite well, but need not be on friendly terms as a result of this. Either circumstance can make it difficult to generate open and honest discussion on what they might hitherto have regarded as their own personal opinions. The relationship between personal and professional morality, or between personal morality and philosophical ethics may therefore require some explanation.
- Students often approach ethics with an initial expectation that there will be a correct answer to each question posed. It is important to help them come to terms with the fact that there will not always be correct answer but instead, one requiring personal judgement.

Preparing students in advance so that they know what to expect from the course and of themselves is advisable. Part of this preparation should focus on the formal structure and conventions of the learning and teaching environment. The preparation needed will depend to a large extent on the nature and content of the course but three key areas that should be considered are safety, mutual respect, and confidentiality.

Safety

It is important for the teacher to have what Bielby calls 'emotional intelligence', *i.e.* the ability to recognise the way in which contentious moral issues can affect people, especially when they impinge on some aspect of personal experience[104]. As private individuals we can refuse to participate in a debate if it distresses us, either by remaining silent or by walking away but when beliefs and values are considered within the context of an ethics class, students might regard themselves as being obliged to remain. This sense of obligation can arise from a fear of 'causing a scene' or losing face by reacting differently from the peer-group, or from a concern that failure to complete the class will result in a lower mark for their coursework. A similar concern can arise in the context of written work that requires students to draw on their own experience.

It is therefore worth considering whether students can be given the right to opt out from topics that they find distressing. Opt-out may be made available for any topic on the course, with the actual omissions being determined in the first instance by the student, subject to approval by those responsible for ensuring that the course learning and teaching objectives are met. Alternatively, where it is possible to predict in advance which areas are of particular sensitivity, opt-out can be limited to those areas.

'Opt-out' can mean that students simply leave out that portion of the course, or that they are guided in the selection of an alternative topic that will meet the course learning and teaching objectives.

Where opting out is considered an acceptable option for students, it will only be effective if students are made aware of this right, and given a mechanism through which they can feel comfortable about exercising it.

In some cases withdrawal might not be considered acceptable. This is not to say that a student will be 'forced' to comply, but rather that a student who opts out will, *ceteris paribus*, be deemed to have performed less effectively than one who remains. There are a number of reasons why it might be difficult to allow a student to opt out. Students could be required to participate because:

All links are available live at http://www.prs-ltsn.ac.uk/ethics

[104] Bielby, P. (2003) 'Courting Controversies: using insights from a legal philosophy course to develop practical recommendations for realising pedagogical objectives in teaching morally contentious issues', *Teaching in Higher Education*, Vol. 8, No. 3, 2003, pp. 369–381

- The ability to retain a level of detachment or objectivity when discussing moral questions is a stated learning objective.
- There is concern that a right to withdraw could be abused by students who are unwilling to complete all portions of the course for other reasons such as a heavy workload.
- Frequent exercise of a right to opt out could result in the student failing to reach the benchmarked requirement for ethics.
- The issue is one that students will have to face when they come to practice their chosen profession. This would be of particular importance in vocational courses where the student's probable future working environment is known.

Where a right of withdrawal cannot be offered there will often be other support mechanisms that students can be made aware of should they need help or advice in dealing with issues raised. For example, students could be given a handout at the start of the course with contact details for:

- University Students' Counselling Services
- University Chaplaincy
- Professional Bodies offering counselling services (these will be of relevance mainly to CPD courses or vocational undergraduate courses in which participants have the option of taking out student membership of a professional association. For example, The Royal College of Nursing offers its members professional and confidential counselling by appointment, either by phone or face-to-face at various RCN offices throughout the UK[105])
- Internet Services such as Ahead 4 Health, an online counselling service based at the University of Leeds.[106] This website also has a useful list of national links.

Mutual Respect

The rules of debate for an ethics class are normally more constrained than they would be for an informal discussion between friends and family. Assumptions will be challenged and arguments scrutinised for coherence and consistency. Some students will find it difficult to accept criticism in areas that affect personal value systems, or which threaten their sense of self-identity. A general atmosphere of mutual respect and tolerance is a desirable aim but is more readily stated than achieved. It is important that the rules of discussion are explained clearly, and that the teacher/facilitator is sufficiently experienced to recognise when student behaviour falls outside that

All links are available live at http://www.prs-ltsn.ac.uk/ethics

[105] http://www.rcn.org.uk/whyjoin/personalsupport.php
[106] http://www.leeds.ac.uk/ahead4health

framework, and respond to it appropriately. In defining the rules or framework for discussion, attention should be paid to the following:

Cultural and Religious Sensitivity

The student body will often be multicultural and multi-faith so consideration should be given to the background ethos of the discussion environment. This is of particular importance if participants are to be asked to set aside cultural and religious appeals when justifying beliefs and courses of action.

A secular rationalist framework for ethics discourse can be as beneficial to a person of deep religious faith as for the secular humanist in so far as it allows them both to investigate how far a moral position can be supported without appeals to tradition, canonical texts or belief in God. However, it can produce tensions within the discussion when there are some participants for whom the secular, rationalist framework is the norm, and others for whom it represents a significant departure from their accustomed way of tacking moral questions.

The difficulties attendant on recognising and respecting cultural or religious perspectives may be more acute within Professional than Applied Ethics frameworks. Applied Ethics students need only adopt a secular framework as a temporary learning methodology. The spiritual, religious and cultural perspectives left outside the classroom door at the start of the class can be collected and reapplied at its close (unless, of course, the student's own learning experience has resulted in a change of belief). For students of Professional Ethics, in so far as the stated learning objectives focus on shaping professional behaviour, the framework adopted as a learning method will also act as a *modus operandum* for real-life ethical decision-making. This can often mean that the secular perspective imposed within the class is put forward as a component of their professional moral identity. A clear and transparent statement of the approach chosen and the reasons for imposing it (for example, by reference to legal obligations and Professional Codes) will facilitate constructive debate.

Bielby notes that if a student expresses a moral view but then refuses to submit that view to further scrutiny, the teacher will be faced with competing pedagogical objectives:

They can show respect to the student, by respecting their wish not to discuss the matter further, but at the risk of leaving other student's feeling frustrated that they have not been allowed to explore the matter further

They can give priority to the values of critical enquiry by facilitating a debate on the issue but at the risk of creating an 'oppressive' environment for the student thus compelled to hear criticism of a deeply held belief. [107]

Guidance on awareness of Religious Perspectives can be found in the Faith Guides to be published by the subject centre for Philosophy, Theology and Religious Studies in 2004.

Multiple Perspectives

Multiple perspectives can arise from differences of culture, religion, social class, gender or academic discipline. This diversity can be advantageous in group discussion-based teaching formats by exposing students to a range of views but when several students within the group share a perspective the discussion can break down into a contest between rival 'factions' and can also lead to the isolation of students whose perspective is not shared by any other group member. A clear framework can be helpful here by ensuring that:

- Every member of the group has an opportunity to speak.
- Views can be expressed without interruption.
- Criticisms are aimed at arguments and not individuals.
- There are mechanisms for defusing heated situations.
- Participants are encouraged to apply constructive criticism to their own beliefs
- Participants are encouraged to look for common ground between opposing views
- Teaching materials are selected for their accessibility to a range of viewpoints.

For similar reasons, drawing students from different disciplines can greatly improve the effectiveness of ethics seminar/discussion groups by exposing students to different personal and professional perspectives and to divergent points of view[108]. These differences of perspective can have a direct impact on the student's learning experience but the relative sizes of different professional subgroups can be critical, as can the skills of the teacher/facilitator. The internal dynamics of such groups are likely to affect the students' learning experience. For example, interdisciplinary healthcare ethics seminars will differ from single-discipline format in a number of ways:

All links are available live at http://www.prs-ltsn.ac.uk/ethics

[107] Bielby, P. (2003) 'Courting Controversies: using insights from a legal philosophy course to develop practical recommendations for realising pedagogical objectives in teaching morally contentious issues', *Teaching in Higher Education*, Vol. 8, No. 3, 2003, pp. 369–381

[108] Tugcu P, Hung R.J, Pan H.L, Nolan P.W, Smith J. (1995) "Ethical awareness among first year medical, dental and nursing students", *International Journal of Nursing Studies*, vol. 32, no. 5, pp. 506-517(12)

- Profession-relative variations in embedded or implicit value-sets are more likely to be recognised and addressed in interdisciplinary groups. In a study of in-hospital ethics seminars carried out by Alderson *et al*, "*[a]haematologist noted the frequently discussed contrast between geneticists offering choice and other clinicians recommending best treatment:* 'The neonatal team have to think about best care, whereas in genetics the ethical goal is more informed choice, when you don't impose your view.'"

- Professional relationships operate within a hierarchy of power and authority that sometimes makes it difficult for junior or subordinate members of staff to express moral concerns[109]. Interdisciplinary groups can be used to explore the extent to which different professions have differing attitudes to authority and its relevance to moral responsibility.

- Professions often show differing gender profiles[110]. Interdisciplinary groups can help to avoid gender imbalances in discussion groups, thus facilitating a broader perspective on gender-sensitive issues.

Nursing and paramedical staff often spend more time with their patients than doctors, and converse with them in a way that goes beyond the medical details of their case. The extent to which the professional develops a 'relationship' with a patient can influence their views on issues such as the patient's ability to offer informed consent and their quality of life. Interdisciplinary groups encourage an understanding of these different perspectives, and can be used to develop ways of reaching inter-professional consensus.

Objectivity versus Emotional Engagement

It can be dangerous to allow students to personalise the issues under discussion as this may arouse feelings of guilt and a need for self-justification. It is not inappropriate for students to be given some mechanism for addressing such issues and ethics modules might be a good place to publicise the existence of that mechanism but this does not mean that the ethics class itself is a suitable forum for students to address morally problematic aspects of their own experience. Where there is a demand for this kind of support a properly constructed self-help group or access to external support services (see the section on Safety above) should be considered as an alternative.

All links are available live at http://www.prs-ltsn.ac.uk/ethics

[109] Alderson P, Farsides B, Williams C. (2002) "Examining ethics in practice: health service professionals' evaluations of in hospital ethics seminars", *Nursing Ethics* vol. 9 no. 5 pp. 508-521(14)

[110] For example, women currently comprise 36% of the veterinary profession (RCVS News, November 2002) but 80% of UCAS 2003 applications from students wishing to study veterinary medicine were from women 2003 (RCVS News, March 2003).

Students will normally be required to maintain a degree of emotional distance to the issues under consideration. The level of detachment required should be determined by the teacher with reference to their stated learning objectives and the teaching materials to be employed, and should be reflected in the discussion framework.

A highly theoretical approach will militate against personal involvement but can lead to too much distance from the issues and a failure to engage in moral dilemmas as real challenges. It is most suited to modules in which the learning objectives emphasise conceptual analysis and reasoned argument.

Practice-based learning allows students to relate the ethical issues under discussion to their own personal experience. It is subject to the danger of excessive personal engagement mentioned above but can be suited to more experienced students, or those for whom the ability to maintain a degree of objectivity or distance on ethical issues is a key learning objective. It can also be appropriate in courses that aim to develop or enhance empathy.

Narrative based learning can also be a good way of helping students maintain a balanced approach (see p. 53 for a more detailed discussion of teaching ethics through narrative).

Confidentiality

When using Contextualised Scenarios or Case Studies drawn from real life there are three main groups whose confidentiality must be maintained:

1) The seminar participants.
2) Professionals involved in the cases under discussion
3) Service-users or other members of the public involved in the cases under discussion.

When using pre-prepared case studies or contextualised scenarios it should be possible to define them so as to protect groups 2 and 3 (if it is not, then the case should not be used) but confidentiality will be more difficult to maintain when students are invited to supply material drawn from their own experience particularly if this is done in a spontaneous or *ad hoc* way rather than as the result of pre-seminar preparation.

Changing the names of any real people mentioned in a case study will be necessary unless the full details of the case are a matter of public record. This makes issues that have been brought before the Courts a good source of teaching material. For cases drawn from other sources confidentiality should be maintained. The General Medical Council's Ethical Guidance on confidentiality in materials used for education and training states that while:

'[d]isclosure of information about patients for purposes such as ... use in education or training ... is unlikely to have personal consequences for the patient ... you should still obtain patients' express consent to the use of identifiable data or arrange for members of the health care team to anonymise records'.[111]

Changing the names will not always be sufficient to prevent identification of the real people involved. For example, if the case is drawn from a workplace of which students have some prior knowledge, they might be able to identify members of staff from details of their position in the workplace, their personal characteristics and idiosyncrasies or their values and beliefs. Similarly, the students might have come to hear of the case through work placements and be able to identify the service-user or staff involved from other aspects of the case (this is more likely for cases selected for discussion because of their distinctive or controversial nature).

Maintaining confidentiality for those involved in real cases will therefore require some knowledge of the background of the participants in the seminar, to determine the depth of 'disguise' that must be applied. When cases are offered spontaneously, this level of preparation will not be possible and confidentiality will require the seminar participants to work to general rules and safeguards designed to protect confidentiality. Healthcare students will often be used to working within this framework. For example, student nurses will normally be issued with a handbook applicable to the whole of their training in which the rules governing confidentiality are specified clearly. Students coming to an ethics seminar with some experience of work placements may be used to participating in case study meetings where confidentiality rules apply, and will simply need to be reminded that ethics seminars are not exempt from normal good practice in this respect.

However, when students (and teachers/facilitators) are not accustomed to professional/service-user relationships a more detailed statement and explanation of the rules might be needed. There is also a wider question concerning examples offered by students from their own personal (as opposed to professional) lives. This might include the experiences of friends or family members who would not normally be accorded the confidentiality rights of the professional/service-user relationship, but should be afforded the same protection as other subjects within the context of a learning and teaching environment.

The confidentiality of seminar participants can be protected by the adoption of the *Chatham House Rule* which reads as follows:

All links are available live at http://www.prs-ltsn.ac.uk/ethics

[111] 'Confidentiality: Protecting and Providing Information', **http://www.gmc-uk.org/standards/default.htm**

When a meeting, or part thereof, is held under the Chatham House Rule, participants are free to use the information received, but neither the identity nor the affiliation of the speaker(s), nor that of any other participant, may be revealed.[112]

However, it should be borne in mind that some students might express an unwillingness to observe Chatham House Rules, perhaps because they would feel obliged to act on any information re illegal acts that might be revealed in the course of a class. Teachers need to be prepared to respond appropriately, to maximise contributions in a way that does not threaten confidentiality.

All links are available live at http://www.prs-ltsn.ac.uk/ethics

[112] http://www.riia.org/index.php?id=14

Future developments

Conflicting professional values can only serve to undermine public faith in professional standards, so an effective learning and teaching strategy must seek to present moral issues in a way that anticipates and fosters dialogue between different professions and between professions and the public. However, this is more easily said than done, and within any programme that incorporates applied or professional ethics there are many important questions to be asked.

Much of this guide has been devoted to a consideration of the ways in which Higher Education seeks to raise professional standards and promote 'good' professional behaviour. However, these primary learning and teaching objectives are themselves controversial.

Should Higher Education concentrate on the enhancement of rational and analytical faculties, leaving the inculcation of professional virtues to the professional bodies, or should it promote sets of values and codes of behaviour?

This in turn raises the issue of whose interests learning and teaching in ethics is intended to serve. Higher Education in general meets a number of social needs, but as the provider of a high quality Learning and Teaching environment, its service-users are the students and it is normally their interests that inform course structure and content. The case of Professional Ethics is less clear cut.

For example, if a nurse is faced with a moral dilemma, there are a number of potential stakeholders to consider when evaluating the various courses of action available to him/her:

- The needs of the patient.
- The professional consequences for the nurse.
- The personal and emotional consequences for the nurse.
- The impact on colleagues
- The impact on the nursing profession as a whole.
- The impact on society as a whole.

There is potential for conflict between these competing interests and the relative weight that the teacher attaches to them has significant learning and teaching implications. It is therefore important that ethics teachers give overt consideration to their primary purpose. Is it to:

- Help the student find fulfilment in their future career by helping them to make moral choices that they can live with, and by reducing the emotional and psychological stress caused by moral indecision and confusion?
- Ensure that the student acts in a way that serves the best interests of society in general and their service-users in particular?
- Ensure that the student acts in a way that serves the best interests of their chosen profession?

Of course, it will sometimes be possible to serve all these interests at once, but where they conflict, difficult decisions must be made. Should Higher Education Institutions be trying to produce particular kinds of people, or should they focus on the increase and promulgation of knowledge? If it is right for Higher Education to aim at producing good professionals why should it stop there? Should they also aim at producing good citizens and if so, where does this leave those who are unwilling or unable to participate in Higher Education?

These are difficult questions but they are worth asking if ethics learning and teaching is to evolve in a way that facilitates the broad societal aims and aspirations that are driving the spread of this subject beyond its traditional base in the humanities.

More opportunities should be sought to reflect on the way in which professional ethics is developing. An open and constructive debate between those concerned with this challenging but vital subject would help to ensure that that public confidence grows hand-in-hand with professional morale. Teachers of moral theory have much to offer in that enterprise, but their expertise will be of greater benefit when it is applied in concert with contributions from those whose subject specific knowledge includes a profound understanding of the contexts in which professionals must bring theory to life.

Appendix: Using Case Studies or Contextualised Scenarios

A stated output for the ETHICS Project was an online case study (or contextualised scenario) resource for teachers. The reason for selecting case studies was that it is a teaching resource used across the disciplines. Contextualised Scenarios or Case Studies are working examples of applied ethical problems used in teaching to highlight relevant ethical principles which are:

- Defined in relation to stated learning and teaching objectives.
- Of proven effectiveness in meeting those learning and teaching objectives.
- Drawn from a wide range of disciplines but presented so as to facilitate translation into other subject areas.

As the case studies presented in this guide have indicated, what counts as a case study, how it is presented and the learning and teaching objectives it serves will vary considerably.

For more case study teaching resources see the ETHICS Project's website at **http://www.prs-ltsn.ac.uk/ethics**

In the example provided in the pragmatic approach, the case study is presented as an extract from a research proposal. It could be used as it is, to highlight an area of particular concern to Research Ethics Committees (namely the use of animals as experimental subjects), or it could be expanded into a complete research proposal outline, with appropriate scientific detail, so that students can begin the more complex process of evaluating the scientific merits of the research and weighing them against the costs in terms of animal experimentation.

That same outline could also be expanded with the detail necessary for students to role-play an application, with some acting as scientists, some as REC members and others as animal rights campaigners.

Alternatively, it could be presented in a context that highlighted the reasoning behind the principles of reduction, replacement and refinement and used as a learning and teaching resource for the theoretical approach.

The scenarios employed in the other two case studies could be similarly represented to serve the needs of different approaches.

Provided the teacher is clear about their objectives, and the way the case study operates to serve those objectives, material can be tailored to meet the needs of the subject area, the expected level of experience (of both student and the teacher), and practical constraints such as group size and number of teaching hours.

Case Studies as Projects

Case studies can be offered to students as projects, to be tackled either individually or by groups of students. This can be of great benefit, especially if students have an opportunity to devote a number of weeks to the project. However, care must be taken to ensure that the group composition, in terms of both background and level, is appropriate to the demands of the case study selected.

Teaching via case study project can be used to develop a number of key skills:

- Time Management
- Presentation and Practical skills
- Research
- For Group work on Case Studies it also helps with:
  - Defining different roles
  - Group dynamics
  - Handling of uneven workloads
  - Resolution of conflict

Case studies can also be used to give students an insight into the roles they can have when they leave university, by exposing them to visiting experts who also function as role-models. These visiting experts can be invited to set up case studies or problems that student groups must solve by working together, and to evaluate the end result. The visitors may need training in order to perform their role effectively, especially if they are not actively involved in teaching outside their role as visitor. This training should cover:

- Conceiving an appropriate case studyconcentration on current issues.
- How to write up the case study for presentation to the students
- Assessment and Providing Feedback to students

This process may help to develop links between the department and potential employers. Visitors get a chance to see how the department works, form a relationship with the staff and assess the quality of teaching the department provides. Individual students who show promise in their execution of the case study might be targeted as future employees.

Group assessment of case study projects can be done by a variety of means:

- Student questionnaires
- Peer-tutor focus groups
- Lecturer's perceptions
- Student Marks and Attendance records[113]

All links are available live at http://www.prs-ltsn.ac.uk/ethics

[113] Further information can be found on www.cases.bham.ac.uk/group. This material has been developed for metallurgy and materials but much of it can be adapted to the needs of applied ethics learning and teaching.